Gray's Wild Game Cookbook
A MENU COOKBOOK

Gray's Wild Game Cookbook
A MENU COOKBOOK

by Rebecca Gray with Cintra Reeve

Photography by Frank Foster
Watercolors by Thomas Aquinas Daly

1983
Gray's Sporting Journal
South Hamilton, Massachusetts

GSJ

Library of Congress Catalog Card Number 83-082973
International Standard Book Number 0-9609842-1-6
Published by   Gray's Sporting Journal Incorporated
                42 Bay Road
                South Hamilton, Massachusetts 01982
Printed in the United States of America

For Edward
And nothing more need I say.
RCG

Acknowledgments

It is almost insulting to acknowledge Cintra Reeve because this book is as much hers as it is mine. But her energy, creativity and inspiration must be emphasized and reiterated. She, quite simply, made this book possible and I thank her.

Many, many thanks to Lou Crawford who not only spent many hours on the phone with me talking over game care from a food technologist's viewpoint, but happens to be an inspirational cook himself. An especially nice characteristic for a father to have.

Very special thanks to Larry Taylor and Frank Foster who made this book beautiful and managed it under deadlines that only true professionals could meet. Thanks to Ted and Donna Williams who spent more hours than I'd like to know about proofreading the manuscript. Thanks to Pat Dunlea and Maggie Murphy who always make food look glorious in a photograph.

Thanks to Bob Elman at Winchester Press for pushing the idea of a *Gray's Wild Game Cookbook* and who would have been my choice for editor had we not decided to publish the book "in house." Thanks to Gerry Quinn at Remington Arms, Angus Cameron at Knopf, and Bill End at L. L. Bean for unselfishly sharing marketing information.

Thank you, too, to Penny Reneson, Joan Ashley, Charley Waterman, John Hewitt and Sig Buchmayr for contributing, consciously or unconsciously, to my thoughts about hunting, cooking and cookbooks.

A professional thanks to those cooks who have lent us their ideas or recipes—Laura Brennan, Zack Hanle, Alice Waters, Judith Olney, and Marcella Hazan.

A final note of thanks to Hope, Sam, William and Ed Gray and to Louie Rossi for never complaining.

Contents

Chapter III — Water Fowl 119

The Main Dishes:

Preface

Cooking and eating wild game is both intimidating and exhilarating. This book hopes to put into perspective the scariness and emphasize the exhilaration.

Hunting and wild game preparation were not a tradition in my family. But I had grown up in a family of Chicago meat-packers; had seen the seven blue stomachs of a steer fall on the floor of a Kansas City slaughter house, smelled a chicken rendering plant in Iowa and watched films of pig's lips mushed up and squirted into hotdog casings. Even still I was not prepared for a feathered, slightly bloody carcass in my kitchen. I prided myself on the early development of a sophisticated palate and had willingly tasted turtle steak, whale meat and fish tongues, but I was uneasy when I took my first bite of woodcock. And if apprehension over their sight and taste were not enough, the creatures also seemed impossible to cook. What cookbooks I could find on game didn't seem to speak to me: Does sour cream have to be in every recipe? Am I told to use a meatgrinder because the author's never heard of a food processor? Has the author tasted a goose smoked for six hours? What vegetables go with bear?

In the ten years since that first feathered carcass, more experience has lessened my apprehensions. Learning to hunt, being involved in the production of the cooking feature for *Gray's Sporting Journal*, experimenting with countless critters, and exchanging ideas about cooking game with outdoor writers, artists, hunt club cooks, outfitters, gun manufacturers, caterers, and ardent gourmands has brought the experience, adjusted the fright, and made possible this cookbook.

There should be more gourmet game cookbooks. If for no other reason than the increased interest in gourmet cooking and in natural foods. Julia Child, Pierre Franey, and Craig Claiborne all carry game recipes in their books and newspaper columns. *Gourmet* magazine yearly prints recipes for game. It was the food of kings and remains the epitome of elegant dining and culinary expertise. Never a trace of injected tenderizers or supplements does a wild animal see, making it the ultimate natural food. It also is high in protein and lower in cholesterol-producing fat than any other meat, and usually has fewer calories.

A chicken's life and diet is highly predictable and rather boring; so is eating or cooking a chicken. It is precisely because the bald-headed chicken man has never regimented waterfowl or upland birds into the "oven stuffer" routine that the exhilaration and to some extent the fear will always remain in wild game cooking.

Wild is what the game animal's life is; a partridge may have feasted on wild grapes, a Canada goose summered in the clean air of Labrador, and the ducks nibbled on Minnesota's wild rice. The duck may also have nearly starved to death on the Ipswich mud flats and been forced to eat a meager diet of crustaceans. All of these elements affect flavor and, for the most part, remain a mystery to the chef and the guests until the tasting reveals it.

If ten years experience were sixty years, I still would cook a black duck for precisely fifty minutes and worry a little that when served he wouldn't taste quite right.

Taste is a matter of taste. Just as we don't know where the dinner has come from, we don't know where our guests are coming from. Those who prefer well-done lamb will also probably prefer well-done venison. My tastes, and thus the basis for the menus in this book, have always drifted toward the classic French and Italian methods of cooking and eating. This is perhaps why Cintra Reeve's techniques appealed so to me. Well-schooled at Madelaine Kamman's "Modern Gourmet" chef school, Cintra was my cooking teacher and provided me with some of my first techniques for game application. As can happen with good learning/working situations, Cintra and I also became good friends. And just as creating this book would have been impossible without Cintra's technical knowledge and professional style, it additionally became a true joy with Cintra.

The taste and style of the cooking along with the presentation of the complete menus are here to implant a sense of security in the unfamiliar. The reader's own sophistication and ability will not be insulted. On the contrary. My hope is that the book will be the inspiration for more experimentation and creativity and will produce another wild game cookbook.

Gray's Wild Game Cookbook
A MENU COOKBOOK

Venison

Several years ago our very well-known writer friend, Charley Waterman, came to visit us. So knowledgeable, so lucid, so funny, he was the ideal for the role of hunter/writer's mentor. Not that I was either a hunter or writer, but at that point I sure aspired to be. I could have easily spent every waking moment beside Charley listening to his stories and never tire of it. Driving through the wilds of the Boston city streets, I picked his brain on everything from the anti-hunters and the rationale for killing to how a husband goes about teaching a wife to enjoy hunting. I had saved my favorite topic for last, wishing to savor the subject and perhaps take notes: Cooking Game. What was Charley's favorite recipe, how long did he and Debie cook a duck, how long did they hang their venison for? It all came spewing forth to get the simple reply, "We don't do much of anything to our game, just cook it."

Penny Reneson had exemplified for me much about how to be the wife of a habitual hunter. When to consider calling the forest ranger if he's over-due; when to assert your own desires to hunt; when to stay at home with the children—all those moments of quandary. Penny seemed instinctually to know how to deal with all of them and I admired her for the ability. We rode to a Ducks Unlimited dinner and I questioned her on the subject I thought would be explosive: Game Cooking. "We don't do much of anything to our game, just cook it."

Of course, when pressed, both Charley and Penny had some quite definite ideas about game cooking, but nonetheless there was a message to be had: The best result is when you don't do anything but cook it. And, however incongruous a statement that might seem in a game cookbook, it is true. It is also why we have tried to keep our recipes and menus simple. Our accent in this book is on the ingredients, not on the complexity of the recipes. But in the acquisition of ingredients we have not sought simplicity nor have we spared the reader's time or money.

Last hunting season was the first in many years that we were forced to hunt ducks without a dog. Our five-year-old golden had died suddenly and mysteriously of a kidney ailment during the summer months leaving us without a trained retriever for duck fetching. Quite cleverly, I simultaneously became pregnant with our third child and too fat to wear waders. Ed was left to face duck season by himself. He arrived home later than usual one morning with one black duck in hand and slightly chagrined. He explained that he had had to strip on the marsh and dive into the icy water in order to retrieve the beyond-wader-reach bird. We do go to great lengths. Cold and wet and fatigue and time and life and death are forever part of it.

It is important for the cook to remember what has gone before. To become cavalier is at best tactless. Ordering up the good green olive oil in advance, making the veal stock from scratch, watering the sage plant every week, spending the extra dollars on liqueurs are our part of it.

And if it seems at times to be too much for too little, just be happy you don't have to jump bare into icy water during October to swim for the duck.

In the olden days (like Robin Hood old days) the word venison referred to any game, not just deer. We have not been that liberal with the word, but do use it in its broader sense to mean all that are in the deer family: Caribou, moose, elk, antelope, white-tail and mule deer. (This is a cook's taxonomy, not a biologist's.) So all of the venison recipes in this chapter are applicable to these animals. Some slight adjustments in quantities of accompanying ingredients and cooking times should be made to accomodate for a larger size (moose, elk) cut of venison.

Chateaubriand Butter with Venison Burgers
Fried Bread
Vegetable Salad
Fresh Fruit

Serves four

Venison burger is not only delightful to eat, but often your best alternative for the cuts damaged in the field or naturally tougher. If the outfitter
has not butchered the deer for you and you fancy doing it yourself, you may
find it difficult getting the meat made into burger. If you are a city-dweller
and hunting refers to what shoppers do at Bloomies or Macy's rather than
something that goes on in the woods, chances are you will not find a butcher
who will grind the meat for you. Even the *la de da* butchers who have
gouged you for years and theoretically owe you a favor are bound by the
state sanitary codes and don't like to risk any infringement of the law.
Rural butchers arc likelier to be able to handle your request to grind the
meat and add the pork fat necessary to create burger. If you are going to try
to grind it yourself, I make two suggestions. Try to use the meat free of any
fat or sinew. And a food processor works better than a hand-crank meat
grinder . I once spent a tearful evening, when I was pregnant with our
third child and Ed was off hunting, trying to jam big chunks of deer leg meat
through a meat grinder. It simply did not work. In general grinding meat at
home is tedious and better to do in small batches or left to the butcher or
outfitter to do. (For more on grinding, see page 209)

CHATEAUBRIAND BUTTER WITH VENISON BURGERS

1 cup white wine
3 shallots chopped very, very fine
1 handful of fresh parsley, chopped
1 tsp. chervil
1 tsp. tarragon
1 cup stock
1 cup (2 sticks) unsalted butter
2 lbs. venison burger (chopped or ground)
Salt and pepper

In a small saucepan combine the wine, shallot, parsley, chervil, and tarragon and bring it to a boil. Reduce heat and simmer very, very slowly until the liquid has been reduced by half. Add the stock and continue to reduce until ½ cup liquid is left. Whip the butter till soft and add the cooled wine and stock mixture. Season with salt and pepper and wrap in plastic wrap. Shape into a log and freeze one hour or overnight. Form the burger into patties and cook over a charcoal grill. Slice several pats of the butter for each burger and serve on top.

FRIED BREAD

1 loaf French bread
½ cup (1 stick) unsalted butter

Slice the French bread into 12 ½-inch pieces and dry them on a cookie sheet in a 300° oven. Do not let them cook. If you wish, rub one side of the dried bread with a garlic clove. In a heavy-bottomed saucepan, melt the stick of butter heating it till it sizzles. Put in the bread and brown both sides. Sprinkle with salt if you like.

VEGETABLE SALAD

1 can artichoke hearts
½ lb. fava beans
½ lb. peas
½ lb. new potatoes

Drain, rinse and quarter the artichoke hearts. Shell, peel and blanch the fava beans. Plunge into cold water. Shell and blanch the peas. Plunge into cold water. When both fava beans and peas are cool combine with the artichoke. Cook the little potatoes in enough salted boiling water to just cover them for 20 minutes. Let cool and then quarter them. Add the potatoes to the other vegetables and then toss with a nice herbed vinaigrette.

Saddle of Venison
Potatoes and Porcini
Braised Fennel
Clafoutis

Serves four

SADDLE OF VENISON

5–6 lbs. saddle of venison
¼   cup olive oil
1   tbsp. lemon juice
    Enough pork lard to cover the
    saddle
1   tbsp. crushed juniper berries
1   tsp. salt
1   onion, sliced
¼   cup red wine vinegar
5   tbsp. unsalted butter
1   lemon
    Sprinkle of flour
    Salt and pepper

Combine the oil and lemon juice and rub over the meat. Let it sit for a couple of hours. Lard with 2-inch strips in even rows with pork fat. Mix the salt and juniper berries together and rub over all the meat. Sauté the onion in a tablespoon of the butter and lay on the bottom of a roasting pan with the meat on top. Add the vinegar to the pan and baste the meat with the remaining butter, melted. Roast in a preheated oven at 350° for about an hour. Then sprinkle the lard with flour and baste with butter. Cook until the lard is crispy.

Julienne the lemon rind and blanch for 5 minutes in boiling water. Combine with the juices from the roast pan and serve on top of the sliced meat.

POTATOES AND PORCINI

    2 oz. wild mushrooms
       (morels.are best,
       otherwise dried *porcini*
       from the gourmet shop)
    3 tbsp. unsalted butter
    ½ cup heavy cream
    1 small garlic clove, minced
    2 lbs. boiling potatoes
       Salt and pepper

Rinse the dried mushrooms quickly in cold water using a strainer so any grit will be removed. Chop coarsely and put in a saucepan with the heavy cream. Simmer very slowly until the cream is reduced to ¼ cup and aromatic with the mushrooms. Sauté the garlic in 1 tablespoon of the butter for a moment and add it to the mushroom/cream mixture. Season with salt and pepper and set aside. Peel the potatoes and slice them into ¼-inch slices. Rinse them twice in cold water letting them sit 10 to 15 minutes each time. Strain and dry potatoes. Butter a low earthenware-type casserole. Put in one layer of potatoes and then one layer of mushroom mixture. Make the last layer potatoes and dot with butter. Season with salt and pepper and bake 20 minutes in a 425° oven.

BRAISED FENNEL

    4 heads fennel
    4 tbsp. unsalted butter
    1 cup stock
    ½ gruyere cheese, grated
       Salt and pepper

Trim, core and cut in half the four fennel heads. Butter a baking dish and arrange the fennel in it. Add the stock and salt and pepper and cover with buttered waxed paper. Cook in a preheated oven at 400° for 30 minutes. Remove the paper and continue cooking for 10 minutes. The stock should have reduced some. Now add the cheese and cook until it is melted and brown.

CLAFOUTIS

2 eggs
¾ cup milk
½ cup flour
   Pinch of salt
1 lb. cherries, pitted (or use any
   good fruit)
1 tsp. vanilla (or grated lemon or
   orange rind)
¼ cup sugar
   Confectioners' sugar

Mix the flour, milk, vanilla or rind, salt, eggs and 2 tablespoons of the granulated sugar together. Butter an oven-proof serving dish and pour a third of the batter in it. Bake that for 10 minutes at 375°. Remove from the oven and add the fruit and sprinkle with the remaining sugar. Pour in the rest of the batter and continue cooking in the oven for 30 minutes. Sprinkle with confectioners' sugar and cut into pie-shaped wedges.

Venison Strip Steaks
Fried Potato Skins
Grilled Red Pepper Salad
Strawberry Ice Cream

Serves four

One of the disadvantages of writing a cookbook so strongly stressing technique rather than concoction is that occasionally words simply do not describe. Such is the case when trying to communicate "doneness" of meat. Cooking time is always an approximate in cookbooks, especially when game is concerned, and should not be taken as the gospel. Try pressing the meat to see if it has a springy touch to it; then it's done. Wiggle a leg to see if it's loose; then it's done. Or cut into it if you're uncertain (better a slice in it than to serve it too rare or over-cooked). Enviable is Cintra's ability to smell doneness. Experience and using your senses are a more reliable guide to determining if dinner is ready than what is printed in these pages, as much as I hate to admit it. We have put cooking times in only as a general guide on how long to gauge the cocktail hour. But always check for doneness.

VENISON STRIP STEAKS

4 thin strip steaks (about ½ lb.
    each)
2 tbsp. oil
¼ cup cognac
½ cup veal stock
4 tbsp. unsalted butter
16 capers, large ones, loosely
    packed in brine
    Salt and pepper

Pan fry the steaks in oil a minute or two on each side and remove to a plate. Deglaze the pan with cognac and add the stock. Reduce the liquid to ¼ cup liquid and whisk in the butter. Rinse the capers well and add to the sauce. Slice the steak, pour the juices into the sauce and season with salt and pepper. Pour the sauce over the meat.

FRIED POTATO SKINS

5 potatoes
3 tbsp. unsalted butter
½ tsp. chopped garlic (optional)
1 tsp. parsley, chopped fine
    Salt

Peel the skin off the potatoes using a potato peeler or a knife if you wish to retain more of the potato. Fry in the hot butter and garlic until crisp. Sprinkle with salt and the chopped parsley. Season with salt and pepper.

GRILLED RED PEPPER SALAD

        2–3 red peppers
        2   cloves garlic, peeled
        1   cup good green olive oil

   Halve the red peppers and take out the seeds or grill whole. Place them cut-side down on a piece of foil in the broiler and broil them 2 to 3 minutes till they are black. Remove and let cool. Peel the black skin off, remove any seeds and slice the peppers into pieces. Put in a jar with the olive oil and garlic cloves and let stand at least overnight. Toss with lettuce and your favorite vinaigrette. They are good in sandwiches and will last a week.

STRAWBERRY ICE CREAM

        6   cups berries (your ice cream
             will only taste as good as
             the berries used.)
        2   tsp. framboise
        1½   cups medium cream
        4   egg yolks
        ½   cup sugar
             Pinch of salt
             (enough ice and salt for the
             ice cream machine)

   Beat together the egg yolks, sugar, and salt till they are smooth but do not ribbon. Add 1 cup cream and mix well. Put over a medium heat stirring constantly until the custard thickens. Remove from the heat, strain and whisk till cool. Add framboise or vanilla and chill. Purée the strawberries. Blend with the custard and add the remaining ½ cup of cream. Churn in ice cream machine according to the manufacturer's directions. Serve with fresh strawberries on top.

———————————

Venison Stew
Homemade Pasta
Crusted Blueberry and Cream Cake

Serves four

One of the common bonds between those who cook and those who hunt is that both avocations lead to the accumulation of equipment. It is so nice to have exactly the right little tool to accomplish the task either in the field or in the kitchen. It also could send you to the poorhouse. It is very nice indeed to own an electric pasta machine, but it is not necessary to making very good homemade pasta. It is very nice to own a choice of three deer rifles, but you can only hunt with one at a time. Use what you already own and upgrade when you know your passions.

VENISON STEW

3–4 lbs. venison stew meat
2   cups red wine
½   cup vinegar
1   onion, sliced
1   carrot, sliced
    A few parsley stems
8   juniper berries
1   tbsp. salt
1   bay leaf
2   crushed cloves
4   sprigs tarragon
4   tbsp. unsalted butter
¼   lb. pancetta, diced
1½   cup stock (about)
1   tbsp. cornstarch
    Salt and pepper

Make a marinade out of the wine, vinegar, onion, carrot, parsley stems, juniper berries, salt, bay leaf, cloves and tarragon sprigs and let the cubed venison sit in it at least overnight.

Drain the marinade from the meat and reserve it. Dry and brown the meat with the pancetta in butter and then cover by ⅔ with the marinade and stock. Cover first with foil pressed close to the meat and bringing it over the sides of the pot. And then add a lid and simmer for about an hour. Test for doneness with a skewer. Strain the sauce from the meat, discard the bay leaf, and thicken with cornstarch. Season with salt and pepper and reheat with the meat. Serve.

HOMEMADE PASTA

2 cups semolina
1½ cups all-purpose flour
2 eggs
1 tbsp. olive oil
1 tbsp. water
½ tsp. salt
2 tbsp. unsalted butter
2 tbsp. finely chopped parsley

Make a mountain of the semolina on the counter-top, sprinkle the salt on the flour and then make a crater on the mountain. Lightly beat the eggs, water, and oil together and pour into the crater. With a fork bring the flour into the egg mixture slowly until all the flour is moist, then knead into a small ball. Continue to knead for 10–20 minutes until the ball, when sliced through the middle, has almost *no* air bubbles. Then place in a plastic bag and into the refrigerator for at least 1 hour. Cut the ball into six parts. Take one of the pieces and knead it for a few minutes. Flatten with a rolling pin and crank through a pasta machine on the widest setting. Fold the pasta and crank through again. Repeat this five more times. Now put the pasta through each setting on the machine without folding it. Finally cut the pasta and place on a plate and toss with ½ cup all-purpose flour. Repeat the procedure for the remaining pieces of dough.

The pasta may now be left to dry. Of course dried pasta can be stored, or after an hour or so, cooked.

CRUSTED BLUEBERRY AND CREAM CAKE

For the cake:

1   quart blueberries
1⅓ cups all-purpose flour
1   tsp. dry yeast
     Pinch of salt
4   eggs
¾   cup sugar
1   tsp. vanilla

For the syrup:

1⅓ cups sugar
¼   cup water
2   tablespoons Grand Marnier
⅓   cup boiling water

Butter a 10-inch spring-form pan and cut a round of parchment paper (or wax paper) to fit the bottom. Butter the paper, too.

Rinse the blueberries. Set aside.

Sift together the flour, yeast, and salt. (If need be, pulverize the yeast in a mortar before sifting.)

Place the eggs, sugar and vanilla in a large metal mixer bowl. Over a very gentle heat, whisk eggs and sugar until quite warm, but don't allow the eggs to set around the edges. Continue beating by machine until the mixture mounts to a thick, almost white foam that forms a ribbon and has at least tripled in volume. Place a dense but single layer of blueberries into the mold. Pour on half the batter, sprinkle on remaining berries and cover with the rest of the batter. Bake in a preheated oven at 350° for 40 minutes.

Prepare a caramel syrup. Place 1 cup sugar and ¼ cup water in a small heavy pan over medium heat. Stir just until the sugar is dissolved, then leave alone. Let the sugar gently bubble until it starts to turn first to straw, then to deeper shades of yellow and gold and then finally to amber. Remove from heat and cool slightly. Add liqueur and ⅓ cup boiling water to make a pourable syrup.

Test cake for doneness by inserting a knife in the center. It should come out clean. Unmold on a serving platter and pour warm caramel syrup over the blueberried top. Sprinkle a layer of granulated sugar (about ⅓ cup) evenly over the cake and place briefly under a broiler until the sugar crystalizes into a crisp topping. Serve with whipping cream.

Venison Stew with Artichoke Hearts and Sun-dried Tomatoes
Basil Bread
Green Salad
Custard Oranges

Serves four

    One year we were made a present of 50 pounds of venison, already butchered, wrapped and frozen. We didn't know the hunters or the outfitter or the butcher or even from what part of the world the deer came from. It was the first time I realized how valuable it is to be able to listen to the long, drawn-out tales of how the buck got bagged and dragged before you have to go in the kitchen and cook it. Prior to that I had always had the privilege of staring glassy-eyed at the hunter while my subconscious soaked up the pertinent details of how big and old the deer was, how clean was the shot, what type of terrain the deer lived in and I had been rather mechanical in applying that knowledge to my choice of recipes for the meat (see Chapter V on "Game Care"). I learned my lesson; I certainly had a hard time figuring out what to do with those 50 pounds of meat to make them taste decent. If you can't be there yourself, at least ask a lot of questions.

    The following is a recipe I would use on good quality stew meat, either a neck roast from a large deer or the shank roast from a smaller deer, cut up.

VENISON STEW WITH ARTICHOKE HEARTS AND SUN-DRIED TOMATOES

1½ lbs. venison stew meat
    Bouquet garni
4   tbsp. oil
2   14 oz. cans (or two boxes
    frozen) artichoke hearts
1   small onion
1   small carrot
6   tbsp. butter
½   cup sun-dried tomatoes
3   cups good red wine
1   cup stock
1   tbsp. cornstarch
1   tbsp. chopped parsley
1   tbsp. grated lemon rind
1   small garlic clove,
    chopped fine
    Salt and pepper

Brown the meat in the oil and remove from the pan. Chop the onion and carrot and sauté in the pan where the meat was. Return the meat and add the stock and wine to the pot. Bring to a boil and add the bouquet garni and sun-dried tomatoes. Soak the canned artichoke hearts for a while in cold water to remove the brine taste (this is unnecessary if they are frozen) and then add them to the pot. Cover the pan with foil, pressing down so there is no space between the foil and liquid. Put the lid on and simmer for about 20 minutes or until a skewer comes out easily and cleanly from a piece of the meat. When done, drain the juices into a frying pan and thicken with cornstarch. Whisk in the butter and season with salt and pepper. Return the meat and add the parsley, garlic and lemon rind. Check for seasoning and serve.

BASIL BREAD

    3 cups all-purpose flour
    1 pkg. dry yeast
    2 tbsp. basil
    1 tsp. salt

In a medium size bowl mix 1 cup of the flour with the yeast and add enough warm water (not hot water) to make a moist and cohesive ball. Fill the bowl with warm water so the ball is covered. Let sit 5 to 15 minutes until the ball pops to the surface. Meanwhile take the remaining amount of flour (this can be all white flour or a mixture such as ⅔ white and ⅓ whole wheat) and put it on top of the counter. Make a trench in the middle of the pile and add the salt. Reconstitute the basil by pouring a little hot water in with it first and stirring then add it to the flour trench. You will need to add more water, a few tablespoons at a time, fluffing it into the flour with your fingers . The mixture should be slightly cohesive but not wet as the yeast/ flour ball will be quite wet. When the ball has risen to the surface of the water, scoop it out and set in the middle of your pile of flour. Knead the ball and the flour together and continue to knead for 8 minutes or so. Put the dough in an oiled or floured bowl with a towel over it and place in a warm spot to rise several hours or until double in bulk. Punch down and let rise again or shape and bake in a preheated oven at 425° till done (about 35–40 minutes). Remember it can rise and be punched down four times, after that the yeast dies. Also, after the first rising it can be punched down and left to rise slowly overnight in the refrigerator.

CUSTARD ORANGES

    3   egg yolks
    ⅓   cup sugar
    1⅓   cup heavy cream
    1½   oz. Cointreau
    4   large navel oranges

Cut off the top of each orange and scoop out the inside. Rinse and let drain. Beat the egg yolks and sugar together then add the Cointreau. Now whip one cup of the cream until it is stiff. Mix in ⅓ of the whipped cream and then fold in the remaining cream. Fill each orange with the egg-cream mixture and set on a plate in the refrigerator for at least two hours. When ready to serve whip the remaining ⅓ cup cream and put a dollop on each orange top. Dust with cocoa.

Venison with Port
Roast Potatoes
Sautéed Watercress
Peach and Pear Ice with Crystallized Violets

Serves four

It took me years to find out what was meant by a "saddle of venison." I had heard of a rack or a haunch but never a saddle. A saddle of venison is the equivalent of a standing rib roast in beef. It is the middle section of chops left intact to make the premier of roasts. At the point of butchering the saddle can cause the very worst consternation. Whether 'tis nobler to wade through a series of delicious meals of venison chops or to go for the glut of an incredible roast... If you go for the glut we suggest the following recipe.

VENISON WITH PORT

4–5 lbs. saddle of venison
2 cups port
4 carrots
4 onions
  A few parsley stems
⅔ cup unsalted butter
½ tsp. powdered cloves
½ tsp. cinnamon
  Pork lard (enough to cover the
  saddle in 2-inch strips)

Preheat the oven to 500°. Lard the saddle and tie with string to hold in place. Peel and chop fine the carrots, onions and parsley stems. Sauté them all in 6 tablespoons of the butter. Lay the vegetables on the bottom of a roasting pan and put the venison on top. Pour the port over it and cook for about 10 minutes. Lower the heat to 400° and continue to cook for another half hour or so basting every 10 minutes. Remove the meat from the pan, skim off any fat and, on top of the stove, reduce the liquid that's left to about half a cup. Add the cinnamon and clove and whisk in the remaining butter and juices which might have exuded from the sliced meat. Check for salt and pepper and serve over slices of the meat.

SAUTÉED WATERCRESS

3 bunches of watercress
3–4 tbsp. unsalted butter
  Salt and pepper

Take each bunch of watercress and cut into 2-inch lengths (the bunches should be cut approximately into thirds). Sauté the watercress in the hot unsalted butter for a second or two then add the lid for two minutes. Remove the lid, season with salt and pepper and a little more butter, and serve.

PEACH AND PEAR ICE WITH CRYSTALLIZED VIOLETS

      2   lbs. ripe peaches
      2   lbs. ripe pears
      1½ Twelve-ounce jars of peach
          jam
      1½ Twelve-ounce jars of pear jam
          Pinch of salt
          Lemon juice to taste

    Make each ice separately. Heat the peach jam slowly till it has melted.
Skin the peaches and remove the stone. Slice the peaches and purée in a
blender or food processor. Now purée together with the melted jam. Add a
pinch of salt and season with lemon juice to taste. Strain into cake tins and
cover with plastic wrap. Make sure the wrap is flush with the ice, then cover
with foil. Freeze for several hours. Repeat the process for the pear ice. They
should be served together quite soft and garnished with crystallized violets.
(You can buy the crystallized violets in your gourmet shop.)

Venison Scallops
Persillade Potatoes
Green Beans
Tarte Tatin

Serves four

VENISON SCALLOPS

8–10	venison scallops (slice ½-inch pieces of meat from a good cut of roast, like the eye of the round, making sure to cut across the grain).
3	tbsp. oil
	Rind from one quarter of an orange
1	cup stock
¼	cup armagnac
¼	cup plus 1 tbsp. unsalted butter
2	tbsp. coarsely chopped hazelnuts
	Salt and pepper

Toast the nuts in the oven till they are light brown. Wrap in a towel for 10 minutes to create steam and to loosen the skin from the nut, rub off the skins and sauté in oil. Chop fine.

Remove the orange rind (making sure to get no pith) from the orange with a potato peeler and julienne into slivers. Blanch for 5 minutes in boiling water. Rinse, drain and reserve.

Pan fry the scalloped venison in 2 tablespoons of oil for a minute or two on each side. Remove from the pan and set aside. Deglaze the pan with armagnac and then add the stock and reduce the liquid to ½ a cup. Whisk in the butter and season with salt and pepper. Add the nuts and orange slivers and serve over the venison scallops.

PERSILLADE POTATOES

2 large potatoes
2 garlic cloves
½ bunch parsley
2 tbsp. bacon fat or butter
Salt and pepper

Chop the parsley and garlic fine and mix together. Peel and slice the potatoes then sauté them in bacon fat over a medium heat with the lid on for five minutes. Remove the lid and add the parsley and garlic mixture and cook for a few more minutes. Season with salt and pepper and serve.

TARTE TATIN

6 hard golden delicious apples
1 sheet Pepperidge Farm Puff
  Pastry or your own
2 tbsp. unsalted butter
¾ cup sugar, plus a sprinkle
½ cup water
  Sprinkle of cinnamon
  Lightly whipped cream

Peel and slice the apples thinly. Next caramelize the sugar by cooking the water and ¾ cup sugar in a frying pan until it is light brown. Remove immediately from the heat as it will continue to cook and transfer to a cake tin. Spread the caramelized sugar over the bottom and lay the apple slices in concentric circles on top. Only the first layer will show so be sure to make that your best. Dot each layer with butter and sprinkle with sugar and cinnamon. Once the pan is full roll out the pastry and cover the apples with it. Cut a few tiny holes in the pastry to let the steam escape. Cook in the middle of a preheated oven at 450° for 20 minutes. Then turn the heat down to 350° and continue to cook for 30 to 40 minutes. Remove and let cool for a few minutes and then invert onto a serving plate. If it has hardened too much, put the cake tin on a burner and re-melt the caramel. Then invert. Be careful of the extra juice that may run out—this juice may be cooked down, cooled and added to the whipped cream.

Venison Chops with Pignolis and Red Peppers
Pepperoni Bread
Green Salad
Stuffed Oranges

Serves four

As a child unsalted butter made me lose my appetite; it simply did not seem right. As an adult I never use salted butter. Of course, historically salt was added to butter to mask the rancidity. And from what I can tell is still the only reason for adding it to butter save some lurking childhood biases in consumers. Unsalted butter is more expensive but can be justified by treating it as a healthier alternative (who needs more salt in their diet).

VENISON CHOPS WITH PIGNOLIS AND RED PEPPERS

4 venison chops
¼ cup walnut oil
¼ cup pignolis (pine nuts)
2 tbsp. unsalted butter
1 sweet red pepper
Salt and pepper

Cut the red pepper and take the seeds out. Slice into thin strips and sauté in the butter. Sauté the pignolis nuts separately in 2 tablespoons of the walnut oil. Toss the peppers and nuts together and set aside.

Sauté the chops in the remaining walnut oil for a minute or two on each side. Place on plates and add the pepper and nut mixture to the top of each chop. Season with salt and pepper to taste.

PEPPERONI BREAD

    3   cups all-purpose flour
    1   pkg. dry yeast
    ⅔   cup pepperoni, chopped
    1   tsp. salt

In a medium size bowl mix 1 cup of the flour with the yeast and add enough warm water (not hot water) to make a moist and cohesive ball. Fill the bowl with warm water so the ball is covered. Let sit 5 to 15 minutes until the ball pops to the surface. Meanwhile take the remaining amount of flour (this can be all white flour or a mixture such as ⅔ white and ⅓ whole wheat) and put it on top of the counter. Make a trench in the middle of the pile and add the salt. Add the chopped pepperoni to the flour trench. You will need to add more water fluffing it into the flour with your fingers. The mixture should be slightly cohesive but not wet as the yeast/flour ball will be quite wet. When the ball has risen to the surface of the water, scoop it out and set in the middle of your pile of flour. Knead the ball and the flour together and continue to knead for 8 minutes or so. Put the dough in an oiled or floured bowl with a towel over it and place in a warm spot to rise 2 hours or until doubled in bulk. Punch down and let rise again or shape and bake in a preheated oven at 425° till done (about 35–40 minutes). Remember it can rise and be punched down four times, after that the yeast dies. Also, after the first rising it can be punched down and left to rise slowly overnight in the refrigerator.

STUFFED ORANGES

    4 large navel oranges
    1 qt. orange ice or sherbet
       Sprigs of mint

Cut off the top of each orange and scoop out the orange and pith inside. Rinse and let drain. Soften the sherbet or ice and then fill each orange shell. Refreeze and then decorate with sprigs of mint.

———————————

Venison Chops with Mustard Butter
Roast Potatoes with Rosemary
Green Beans and Beet Salad
Coffee Granita

Serves four

In many of the recipes we have listed veal stock as an ingredient. To our knowledge veal stock is not something that can be bought, it can only be made. And although expensive and time-consuming, it is not difficult and is very, very worth doing. Cintra has made it a once-a-month ritual. It is not difficult to do, that I can vouch for, and the 12-hour simmer can even take place while you sleep. And after it has become a part of your life it will be like hunting is. The extra time and effort is simply not remembered, only how good it is. (see page 52)

VENISON CHOPS WITH MUSTARD BUTTER

    4 venison chops
    ¼ cup cognac
    ¼ cup veal stock
    1 tbsp. oil
    1 tbsp. prepared course-grained
       mustard
       Salt and pepper

Pan fry the chops in oil and set aside. Deglaze the pan with cognac and add the veal stock and cream. Reduce to half the quantity, remove from heat, and whisk in any juices that have oozed from the resting chops. Add the mustard. Season to taste with salt and pepper and serve over the chops.

ROAST POTATOES WITH ROSEMARY

  16 little red potatoes
    4 tbsp. melted, unsalted butter
       Rosemary
       Salt and pepper

Paint the potatoes with the melted butter and sprinkle liberally with rosemary. Roast in the oven for about 35 minutes at 350° or until they are tender. Season with salt and pepper.

GREEN BEANS AND BEET SALAD

    1 lb. green beans
    8 medium-size beets
    1 tbsp. vinegar
    1 tsp. prepared mustard
    ½ cup olive or walnut oil
       Splash of soy sauce
       Salt and pepper
       Mint
       Lettuce

Blanch the beans in salted boiling water until they are just tender. Plunge them into ice water to stop the cooking and preserve the color. Drain them and let dry. Steam the beets until they are tender and can be pierced with a fork (about half an hour). Let them cool, peel and julienne them. Make a vinaigrette by combining in a blender the vinegar, mustard, oil, soy sauce, salt and pepper. Pour half the vinaigrette on the beets and half on the beans and toss each separately as the beets will bleed if you toss them too much together. Then toss the two vegetables together gently and serve on a bed of lettuce with a sprig of mint on each serving.

COFFEE GRANITA

1½ cups strong espresso coffee
(Italian roasted)
2   tbsp. sugar

If the coffee is not strong enough let it infuse for ½ hour or so. Then strain. Dissolve the sugar in the coffee and chill. Then freeze in ice trays or a brownie tin, stirring every 15 minutes or so for about 3 hours. Serve immediately with cream or whipped cream. Coffee Granita is not meant to be a solid ice. It should be melt-in-your-mouth texture.

Venison Steaks with Wild Mushrooms
Blue Cheese Polenta
Spinach and Bibb Lettuce Salad
Strawberry Ice

Serves four

In the years of working on the food photography for *Gray's Sporting Journal* I have been continually impressed with the value of attractive food presentation. This is one reason we felt strongly about including the color photographs in this book. What the eye perceives as being luscious becomes so to the taste buds, too. It is an art, and although the photos here are created by professional artists, I have seen equal creativity in the practiced cook. Game, of course, can present its own unique problems for pleasant presentation at the table. But the extra moments spent pulling every feather from the duck legs or taking a pair of tweezers to the venison to remove the last hair is worth more to the insurance of a tasty meal than any exotic recipe.

VENISON STEAKS WITH WILD MUSHROOMS

2 lbs. venison steak
1 tbsp. oil
¼ cup cognac or armagnac
1 oz. dried wild
  mushrooms
1 cup cream
⅓ cup veal stock
  Salt and pepper

Rinse the mushrooms in cold water quickly and put into a pot with the cream. Bring it to a boil and then turn it down to a slow simmer. Continue to simmer until the cream is reduced by half.

Pan fry the steak in the oil and remove to a plate to let rest. Deglaze the pan with cognac and add the veal stock. Bring to a boil and let reduce by half. Add the cream and mushroom mixture and any juices that have exuded from the resting steak and let simmer together for a few minutes. Season with salt and pepper and serve over the sliced meat.

BLUE CHEESE POLENTA

¾ cup cornmeal
1 small onion (optional)
2 cups milk
6 tbsp. unsalted butter
½ cup heavy cream
5 oz. blue cheese, diced
½ tsp. nutmeg
2–3 tsp. kosher salt
  Pepper

If you are using the onion, sauté it in the butter until translucent. Then, in a small saucepan bring the onion, butter and milk to a boil. Add the cornmeal slowly, stirring constantly till thick and the spoon can stand up in it. Be careful as the polenta will spit at you. Now add the cheese, nutmeg and salt. Remove from the heat and beat in the cream and pepper. Turn immediately into buttered muffin tins and let rest till set. Remove from the tin and put in a heavy oven-proof pan and cook at 400° for 15 minutes (if you like, you can add a little more cheese to the tops of the polenta muffins before putting them in the oven.)

STRAWBERRY ICE

     6 cups strawberries (approximately)
     1 cup sugar
        Pinch of salt
     1 tbsp. Kirsch
        (Remember to have enough ice
        and salt for your ice cream
        freezer, too).

Wash and hull the strawberries. Purée in the blender. You should have about 1 quart of purée. Boil half a cup of water and add the sugar and cook for 5 minutes. Let cool. Add the sugar syrup to the fruit juice as needed to please your taste. Add salt and lemon juice to help the taste if need be and then pour in the Kirsch. Chill the mixture in the canister from your ice cream maker. Then freeze according to the ice cream machine's directions.

———————————————

Venison Steaks Marinated
Grilled Red Pepper Salad
Mashed Potatoes with Fresh Basil
Vanilla Ice Cream with Homemade Butterscotch Sauce

Serves four

When we were going through the editing process for this book Cintra wrote all over the manuscript in several places and in big bold letters "remove the bay leaf." Of course, this is an instruction given in every cookbook and I wondered why Cintra was so concerned that it be repeated religiously here. When questioned she said that bay leaves are not digested and their sharp edges can actually perforate the stomach wall. This piece of information made it easier to remember to always put the instruction in the recipes—and take the bay leaf out!

VENISON STEAKS MARINATED

2	lbs. venison steak
2½	cups olive oil
25–30	juniper berries, lightly toasted and crushed
	Juice from 2 lemons (about ⅓ cup) plus the rind finely grated
1	tsp. celery salt
10	peppercorns, crushed
2	tbsp. ground coriander seed
1	bay leaf, crumbled
2	tbsp. unsalted butter
¼	cup cognac
⅔	cup veal stock
½	cup heavy cream
2	tsp. sour cream
	Salt and pepper

In a blender, or with a mortar and pestle, blend the juniper berries, lemon rind, celery salt, peppercorns, coriander seed and bay leaf. Add this to the oil and lemon juice and marinate the steak for four days.

Wipe the steak dry and pan fry it in butter. Remove the meat and let rest. Deglaze the pan with cognac and then add the veal stock. Bring to a boil and reduce ¼ of the liquid. Add the heavy cream and continue to let it boil and reduce. Add any juices that have exuded from the steak while it has been resting and after it has been carved. Remove the sauce from the heat and whisk in salt and pepper and the sour cream. Serve over the steak.

VEAL STOCK

6 lbs. veal shank
3 lbs. veal trimmings
3 lbs. veal bones
3 cups white wine
4 large onions, not peeled, with
  a clove stuck in one
3–4 carrots, peeled
  Salt and pepper
  Parsley Stems
  Bay leaf
  Thyme

In the oven and in several batches, brown the the meat. It is best to do in a large roasting pan. Don't let the bottom burn. Add a little water if necessary as you go along.

Put all meat in a large stock pot. Add the onions, carrots and bones.

In the roasting pan where the meat was browned add the water and wine to cover the dried meat juices. Bring this to a boil on top of the stove scraping the sides and bottom with a whisk. When the juice is just a ½-inch layer on the bottom of the pan add it to the meat.

Fill the rest of the pot with water to cover the meat and vegetables. Bring to a boil and then turn down to a simmer. Add 2 teaspoons of salt, several peppercorns, thyme, bay leaf and parsley stems.

Cook 12 hours adding boiling water as necessary to keep the stock level up. Strain through a colander lined with a wet piece of cheesecloth. Skim off the fat and cook down to ⅓ in quantity and let cool again to room temperture. Freeze in ice cube trays. Once frozen remove with a knife and store cubes in plastic bags.

Do not let the stock sit long at room temperature or it will sour. And *never* let it sit at room temperature with the bones in; always strain them out even if you have to stop the cooking in the middle, only to restart later. Meat stock is fertile ground for bacteria.

GRILLED RED PEPPER SALAD

2–3 red peppers
2 cloves garlic, peeled
1 cup good green olive oil

Halve the red peppers and take out the seeds (or use whole). Place them cut-side down on a piece of foil in the broiler and broil them 2 to 3 minutes till they are black. Remove and let cool. Peel the black skin off, remove the seeds and slice the peppers into pieces. Put in a jar with the olive oil and garlic cloves and let stand at least over night. Toss with lettuce and your favorite vinaigrette. These are good in sandwiches too.

MASHED POTATOES WITH FRESH BASIL

5 potatoes (Idaho or russet)
½ cup (1 stick) unsalted butter
  cut into pats
½ cup heavy cream
  Fresh basil to taste
  Salt and pepper to taste

Wash, peel and quarter the potatoes. Put the potatoes in cold salted water and bring them to a boil and cook till they are soft when you insert a fork, about 20 minutes. Remove them from the water and push through a sieve or potato ricer into a bowl, add the butter and cream and whisk till fluffy. Chop the basil and add it with the salt and pepper to the potatoes and taste.

If you are trying to hold the potatoes put them in a double boiler, uncovered, and save half of the butter and cream to add at the last minute.

HOMEMADE BUTTERSCOTCH

2 cups sugar
¾ cups water
2½ cups hot cream
4 tbsp. unsalted butter (optional)
  Pinch of salt

Make a sugar syrup with the water, sugar, and salt. Cook till light brown. Remove from heat and add the heated cream stirring all the time. For a richer sauce, add the softened butter after the cream.

53

Charcoal Grilled Venison Steaks with Rosemary Butter
Bibb Lettuce and Tomato Salad
White Bean Purée
Coffee Ice Cream and Hazelnut Liqueur

Serves four

In beef the cut of meat identifies for us the quality of the meat. Unfortunately what we have learned is a great cut of beef is not necessarily paralleled in venison. Venison steaks, for example, are quite often the less desirable cut of meat; the chops the best. Nonetheless, you can't go wrong with a charcoal grilled steak.

CHARCOAL GRILLED VENISON STEAKS WITH ROSEMARY BUTTER

                2   lbs. venison steak
                ½   cup (1 stick) unsalted butter
                2   tsp. dried rosemary
                ½   tsp. garlic, chopped
                    Salt and pepper

Chop the rosemary and the garlic very fine. Whip the butter and add the rosemary, garlic and salt and pepper to taste. Wrap the butter in plastic wrap and shape into a log. Place in the freezer while you start the charcoal. Once the coals are burnt down, but still quite hot, cook the steak quickly. Cut slices of the butter to go on top of each serving.

WHITE BEAN PURÉE

                1   lb. white beans, soaked an
                    hour
                2½ cups chicken stock
                2½ cups water
                1   onion
                2   cloves
                1   bay leaf
                    Pinch of thyme
                    A few parsley stems
                    Salt and pepper
                ¾   cup heavy cream
                ½   cup (1 stick) unsalted butter,
                    softened

Drain the soaking beans and pour in the water and broth (if you don't have any chicken stock, all water with chicken bouillon cubes is fine). Peel the onion and push the cloves into it. Add the the onion, bay leaf, thyme, parsley stems and salt and pepper to the bean pot and bring to a boil. Simmer until the beans are tender (about a half hour to an hour). **Remove bay leaf.** In small batches, churn up the bean mixture in a food processor. Zipping it for just a second not to purée, but just to break the skins of the beans. Push through a strainer back into the pot and mix in the butter and cream. Reheat gently and season with salt and pepper.

Grilled Venison Chops with Blue Cheese and Caraway Seeds
Sweet Potato Gratin
Braised Fennel
Fresh Figs

Serves four

GRILLED VENISON CHOPS WITH BLUE CHEESE AND CARAWAY SEEDS

4	chops
½	cup (1 stick) unsalted butter
1	tbsp. blue cheese, crumbled
½	tsp. crushed caraway seeds
	Few drops of Worcestershire sauce
2½	tbsp. oil
	Salt and pepper

Whip the butter till it is soft. Add the cheese, caraway, Worcestershire and salt and pepper and mix well. Roll up in plastic wrap and shape into a log and freeze for at least 1 hour or preferably overnight. Pan fry the chops in oil, about two or three minutes a side (depending on thickness) and place on plates. Slice off two or three pats of the cheese/butter per chop and put them on top to melt over the chops.

SWEET POTATO GRATIN

3   white potatoes
3   yellow sweet potatoes (or yams)
2½ cups cream
     Butter (for greasing the dish)
½   tsp. cognac
¼   tsp. nutmeg
¼   tsp. powdered cloves
     A pinch of thyme
     Salt and pepper

Peel and cut the potatoes into ⅛-inch slices. Layer in a buttered baking dish. Add the cream, clove, nutmeg, thyme and salt and pepper. Bake at 325° for 1½ hours.

BRAISED FENNEL

4   heads fennel
4   tbsp. unsalted butter
1   cup stock
½ gruyere cheese, grated
    Salt and pepper

Trim, core and cut in half the four fennel heads. Butter a baking dish and arrange the fennel in it. Add the stock and salt and pepper and cover with buttered waxed paper. Cook in a preheated oven at 400° for 30 minutes. Remove the paper and baste the fennel, continue cooking for 10 to 20 minutes longer. The stock should have reduced somewhat. Now add the cheese and cook until it is melted and brown.

Venison Steak with Red Wine
Bittergreens and Cheese Salad
Garlic Toasts
Rhubarb Tart

Serves four

All game, because of its high protein content, continues to cook after it has come off the stove. But for some reason I have found it more so with venison than with other types of game. It is worth being aware of—you can always cook something more but not less. Also, not only does game continue to cook, it then loses heat very quickly and becomes cold. We make an extra effort to serve game on warmed plates or platters so it is still warm when it gets to the table.

VENISON STEAK WITH RED WINE

2 lbs. venison steak
2 tbsp. finely chopped shallots
⅔ cup good red wine (the
    better the wine, the better
    the sauce)
½ cup veal stock
6 tbsp. unsalted butter
2 tbsp. oil
    Salt and pepper

Pan fry the steak in oil until done. Remove to a platter. In the pan put one of the tablespoons of butter and the shallots over a medium heat and cook until they are just barely soft. Add the wine and bring to a boil and continue boiling until you have ⅓ left. Add the veal stock and simmer till half of that is left, you should have about ½ cup liquid in all now. Slice the meat against the grain. Whisk in the remaining butter to the sauce and any of the juices from the steak on the platter. Season with salt and pepper and serve the sauce over the steak.

BITTERGREENS AND CHEESE SALAD

Escarole, chicory or arugula
Bibb lettuce
French bread
5 tbsp. unsalted butter
4 strips of bacon
3 oz. Blue cheese
Vinaigrette
Garlic clove
Salt and pepper

Wash and dry the lettuce and break into bite size pieces. Slice the bread into 1-inch square pieces and fry in butter. Rub with garlic and set aside. Cut the bacon into 1-inch pieces and fry till medium done, not crisp. Cut the cheese into cubes. Combine the lettuce, bacon and cheese and toss with the vinaigrette. Add the croutons and check for seasoning. Serve.

GARLIC TOASTS

1 loaf French bread
8 heads of firm garlic
5 tbsp. good green olive oil
Salt and pepper

Cut the French bread into ½-inch slices and toast on a cookie sheet in a 300° oven making sure both sides are lightly browned.

Separate all the garlic cloves, peel and remove any green sprouts. Boil all the cloves in a couple quarts of cold, salted water for 5 minutes. Drain and repeat the boiling process three more times. The garlic cloves should be easily pierced with a fork. Purée the cloves with the olive oil in a food processor or blender or mash with a fork. Add salt and pepper to taste. Spread the garlic purée on the toast and run under the broiler to glaze. Serve.

RHUBARB TART

3 lbs. rhubarb (preferably the
   young sticks)
¾ cup sugar
1 lemon, grated
   Splash of vanilla or sherry
⅔ cup crème fraîche, or a mixture
   of sour cream and heavy
   cream
2 tbsp. confectioners' sugar
½ tsp. powdered cloves
½ lb. pastry

Roll out the pastry into a buttered 9-inch tart or pastry dish and refrigerate for 1 hour.

With a knife peel the thin outer layer from each stick of rhubarb and slice very thinly. Put in a heavy saucepan with the granulated sugar. Cover and cook 15 minutes over a medium low heat. Then remove the lid and turn the heat up to evaporate all the juices. Stir constantly so it will not stick and burn. Once it has become the consistency of jam remove and let cool. Add the lemon rind and a few drops of the vanilla or sherry.

Prick the bottom of the refrigerated pastry shell with a fork and place foil tightly over the pastry. Fill with pie weights or beans and cook on the lower shell of a preheated oven at 425° for 8 minutes. Remove the foil and weights, prick the crust again, sprinkle with a little granulated sugar and return it to the oven for 5 more minutes or until the crust is caramelized. Remove it from the oven and carefully slide the crust onto a cake rack to cool.

Whip the cream and sour cream (or just the crème fraîche) together with the confectioners' sugar and clove. When it's thick, spread it over the bottom of the pastry shell. Then spread the rhubarb over the whipped cream mixture and serve within 30 minutes, otherwise the crust becomes soggy.

Venison Calzone
Sliced Tomatoes with Basil
Fried Sage Leaves
Poached Pears

Serves four

Deer are everywhere it seems. I was particularily impressed with that fact after visiting friends in Connecticut. Ed was on a deer hunt and I had ventured off to a Ducks Unlimited dinner unescorted. Rather than make the trip back to Massachusetts the same evening I stayed the night with friends. In the morning the offer of a quick pass through their back woods in search of deer was made. The concept of potentially shooting a deer in Connecticut while on a morning stroll and with Ed in the Maine woods for a week trying to get his deer tickled my fancy. Dressed improperly in the cocktail attire of the previous evening and allowing only an hour for the hunt, I was amazed to get a glimpse at some twenty good-sized deer in the space of that hour. And we would have had our venison had it not been for some near-sighted shooting on the part of my companion. But as some 122,816,330 pounds of venison are brought to the tables in America annually, variety in recipes is mandatory. This recipe offers a good change of pace from venison loaf or burgers.

VENISON CALZONE

3 cups all-purpose flour
1 pkg. dry yeast
2 tbsp. oregano
1 cup ground venison, sautéed in
   bacon fat with a little onion and
   garlic
½ cup slivered gruyere cheese
1 cup eggplant, chopped and
   sautéed
¼ cup chopped parsley
1 tsp. salt
   Black ground pepper

In a medium size bowl mix 1 cup of the flour with the yeast and add enough warm water (not hot water) to make a moist and cohesive ball. Fill the bowl with warm water so the ball is covered. Let sit 5 to 15 minutes until the ball pops to the surface. Meanwhile take the remaining amount of flour (this can be all white flour or a mixture such as ⅔ white and ⅓ whole wheat) and put it on top of the counter. Make a trench in the middle of the pile and add the salt. Reconstitute the oregano by pouring a little hot water in with it first and then add it to the flour trench. You will need to add more water, fluffing it into the flour with your fingers. The mixture should be slightly cohesive but not wet as the yeast/flour ball will be quite wet. When the ball has risen to the surface of the water, scoop it out and set in the middle of your pile of flour. Knead the ball and the flour together and continue to knead for 8 minutes or so. Put the dough in an oiled or floured bowl with a towel over it and place in a warm spot to rise two hours or until doubled in bulk. Punch down and roll out into a 3″ × 12″ rectangle. Now brown the venison and sauté the eggplant. Put the burger, eggplant and grated cheese in layers in the center of the dough. Then pull the sides of the dough up over the meat mixture and wrap tightly, pinching the seams. Flip over so the seam is on the bottom. Let rise again and bake in a preheated oven at 425° till done (about 35–40 minutes).

FRIED SAGE LEAVES

½ cup large sage leaves
2 tbsp. unsalted butter

Fry the sage leaves in butter until they're stiff but not browned. Remove with wooden tongs and season with salt.

POACHED PEARS

4 ripe pears
2 cups water
1⅓ cups sugar
1 vanilla bean, split
Several drops of lemon juice

Peel the pears with a vegetable peeler and core from the bottom with a melon baller. Rub the peeled pears with lemon juice. In a saucepan combine water, a few drops of lemon juice, and sugar and bring it to a boil. Add the halved vanilla bean and reduce the heat. Simmer for 5 minutes. Then add the pears and continue to simmer for about 10 minutes or until the pears are tender. Remove the pears from the syrup and stand upright on a plate in the refrigerator. The chilled pears can be served with crème anglaise, whipped cream, chocolate shavings, or a liqueur over it.

Venison Chops with Basil Cream
Homemade Pasta with Parsley
Salad with Hazelnut Dressing
Brandied Apricots and Crème Anglaise

Serves four

VENISON CHOPS WITH BASIL CREAM

4 venison chops
1 tbsp. oil
1 tbsp. unsalted butter
1 pint heavy cream
½ tbsp. basil
Salt and pepper

Reduce the cream. Pour the cream into a frying pan, bring to a slow boil and add the basil. Simmer until halved in quantity and thick. If it gets too thick add a little water and stir. Meanwhile cook the chops. Brush away any bone chips left from butchering and remove all fat from the venison. In a frying pan with the hot oil and butter, sauté the chops very quickly, 2 or 3 minutes per side. Remember venison continues to cook long after it comes off the heat. The chops should be pink. In the pan add a little stock or water and deglaze; then add the basil cream. Stir and season with salt and pepper and serve with the chops.

HOMEMADE PASTA WITH PARSLEY

2 cups semolina
1½ cups all-purpose flour
2 eggs
1 tbsp. olive oil
1 tbsp. water
½ tsp. salt
2 tbsp. unsalted butter
2 tbsp. finely chopped parsley

Make a mountain of the semolina on the counter-top, sprinkle the salt on the flour and then make a crater on the mountain. Lightly beat the eggs, water, and oil together and pour into the crater. With a fork bring the flour into the egg mixture until all the flour is moist, then knead into a small ball. Continue to knead for 10 or 20 minutes or till there are no air bubbles when the doughball is cut in half, then place in a plastic bag and into the refrigerator for at least 1 hour. Cut the ball into six parts. Take one of the pieces and knead it for a few minutes. Flatten with a rolling pin and crank through a pasta machine on the widest setting. Fold the pasta and crank through again. Repeat this five more times. Now put the pasta through each setting on the machine without folding it. Finally cut the pasta and place on a plate and toss with ½ cup all-purpose flour. Repeat the procedure for the remaining pieces of dough.

The pasta may now be left to dry. Of course dried pasta can be stored, or after an hour or so, cooked.

For this menu cook the pasta in a large quantity of boiling water for a minute or two. Rinse in cold water the return it to the pan and add the butter and chopped parsley. Toss and season with salt and pepper.

HAZELNUT SALAD

Boston lettuce
½ cup toasted and crushed
    hazelnuts
¾ cup hazelnut oil
3 tbsp. vinegar
1 clove shallot, chopped fine
1 tsp. prepared mustard
Salt and pepper

Wash and spin dry the lettuce. Toast the hazelnuts in the oven. Remove and cover with a tea towel to steam. Rub the skins off the nuts and chop fine. Sprinkle over the lettuce.

Combine the remaining ingredients in the blender and zip on high for a few seconds. Pour over the salad and toss.

BRANDIED APRICOTS WITH CRÈME ANGLAISE

      1 lb. apricots
      3 cups brandy (or enough to cover)

Place the apricots in a jar and cover with brandy. Seal and let stand at least 48 hours. Serve with crème anglaise (see page 182).

Upland Birds

The first time I ever went hunting, it was for upland birds. On a very hot September day in Virginia, we waited under a tree on the edge of a cornfield for dove to fly. It was like all hunting and fishing is—filled with parts that were unique only to that hunt and filled with other parts that were like many hunts—past and future.

We parked the cars and walked a short dirt road that led to the cornfield. Our host, a kind gentleman and father to a friend of ours, with great exuberance raced twenty or so paces ahead of us in obvious excitement over the beginning of his hunting season. A starling fluttered overhead and in an instant the man had raised his gun and pulled the trigger. I remember his wife crying out her husband's name as the little bird fell to the ground and the ring of the shot lingered in the air. For several minutes the novice in me prevented my comprehending what had transpired. And then, with a tremendous flood of horror, I realized what had happened. The wrong bird had been shot. A bird that was not a game bird and never, unless starvation was staring you in the face, to be eaten lay uselessly dead. It was a mistake by a nice man with a puppy dog-like attitude and eyesight that was not what it had once been. But it was a mistake that scratched at my conscience and stayed on my mind.

I realized that purpose had a lot to do with my own willingness to hunt. For me killing an abundant quantity, or for the sport, or just for the sake of a bad mistake had no purpose. But hunting becomes a joy for me when it provides sustenance and requires ability in the field and kitchen.

On the other hand, while I do hope for proficiency in my hunting and cooking, I also don't want any prowess to become pretentiousness.

Ed and I used to hunt a particularly great covert in Dorset, Vermont. As time went on we noticed that the great covert often had a certain Jeep parked at its edge. We asked a local friend about the Jeep and got as a reply a grin and the name of a well-known and highly successful partridge hunter. A year or so later there was an article in *Sports Illustrated* about this same famous hunter and a game of one-upmanship that was played among the Dorset great grousers: To ask a large group of friends over for a big grouse feed and to offer seconds to everybody. That game's not for me. Not only because I'm not that good a hunter but because I'm not that good an eater. Two grouse is too much for me to eat, too much for most people to eat. Game, or any precious food, should be like a good sexual experience: It should be just enough to satisfy but not totally satiate the desire for more.

These are, of course, my own opinions and I state them here so the cook and reader of these menus has a better idea about the design of each menu and the kind of portion and quality control I've laced throughout them. Or, in short, if the slob in you is screaming to be released you'll need to double these recipes and move to Belgium where starling is served in the best of restaurants.

Quail for the Campfire
Grilled Red Onion
Charcoal Grilled Bread
Almond Cake

Serves four

These recipes are designed for you to use the first night of an *ooh la la* camping trip. But of course they can be done right at home either in an oven or on your outdoor grill.

Good, extra virgin olive oil is important to many of the recipes in this book, but particularly to this bread. I recommend ordering some from a catalog if you can't get any at a local gourmet shop.

QUAIL FOR THE CAMPFIRE

4 quail
Fresh rosemary and thyme leaves
or 1 tbsp. each dried rosemary
and thyme per bird
4 bacon strips
Salt and pepper

Salt and pepper the cavity of each bird and stuff with the fresh herbs. Truss and wrap first with a strip of bacon and then with buttered parchment paper or foil (several layers of parchment paper—two of the foil). Place in hot cinders for 35 minutes. Be sure to turn the birds every so often and renew the foil/paper if necessary.

GRILLED RED ONION

2 red onions
2 tbsp. unsalted butter
Salt and pepper

Slice the onions ¼-inch thick and grill them lightly for 2–3 minutes per side either over the campfire or in the broiler. Serve with salt and pepper. Now sauté them quickly in the butter over a medium heat and season with salt and pepper or dribble with a good olive oil for a more salad-like taste.

CHARCOAL GRILLED BREAD

1 loaf of French bread
1 garlic clove
½ cup good green olive oil

Slice the bread into ½-inch pieces and rub each side with the garlic. Grill over a medium-low fire and then pour a little of the olive oil on each piece.

ALMOND CAKE

¾ cup almonds
6 tbsp. unsalted butter
⅔ cup sugar
3 eggs
½ cup sifted all-purpose flour
3 tbsp. brandy
Dusting of confectioners' sugar

Roast the almonds on a cookie sheet in a 300° oven for about 20 minutes or until they are a nice golden tan. Be sure to shake the almonds often while cooking so they do not get over-done. Chop the almonds very fine. This can be done in a food processor if you like.

Melt the butter and when cooled stir in the eggs and sugar. Then add the flour, almonds and brandy.

Butter and flour an 8-inch square pan and pour the batter into it. Bake at 325° for 20 minutes or until a skewer pulls out clean when you stick it in the center of the cake. Let cool in the pan, then cut into squares and dust with the confectioners' sugar.

Green Grape Quail
Wild Rice with Walnuts
Sliced Tomatoes with Fresh Basil
Crème Brulée

Serves four

This menu you might think about using early on in the quail season when the fresh basil and tomatoes are still easily obtainable from a garden or vegetable stand. Nothing is worse in my mind than having to serve those pale orange, hard balls packaged in plastic baskets and cellophane. Don't be scared off by the use of grape leaves in this recipe. They are very often found in chain supermarkets or you can substitute by using foil, although this is, obviously, not as much fun.

The cooking method for the wild rice—that of covering the rice with 3 inches of water and boiling it all without a lid until the water has evaporated—is one that I discovered from an enclosure in a package of the wild grain and works with any amount of wild rice. It also is a method which insures doneness and doesn't involve all that ridiculous soaking which is so often recommended.

The crème brulée suggested here is a more liquid one than is sometimes served. If you like your crème brulée to resemble the consistency of week-old refrigerated Jello you will need to cook this recipe at least twice as long.

GREEN GRAPE QUAIL

4 quail
4 strips of bacon
8 grape leaves
1 lb. seedless green grapes
Butter

Wrap each quail first in bacon and then in grape leaves. Put wrapped quail in a buttered pan and cut a piece of wax paper to fit over the top of the birds. Butter the side of the wax paper which touches the birds. Cover birds with wax paper and a lid and cook at 425° for 15 minutes. Add the grapes and baste the birds with the juices. Cook for 10 minutes more.

WILD RICE WITH WALNUTS

½ cup wild rice
⅓ cup walnuts, chopped
1 tbsp. unsalted butter
Salt and pepper

Toast the chopped walnuts while you cook the wild rice. Cook the rice by putting it in a sauce pan with enough water so it is covered by 3 inches. Bring it to a boil and then simmer it uncovered until all the water has evaporated, about ½ to ¾ of an hour. Add the salt and pepper and butter. Toss in the toasted walnuts and serve.

CRÈME BRULÉE

6 eggs
5 tbsp. sugar
3 cups heavy cream (or 1½ cups heavy cream and 1½ cups whipping cream)
1 tbsp. vanilla
½ to ⅔ cup light brown sugar

Separate the eggs and combine the yolks well with the white sugar and cream. Heat the mixture until very warm over a medium heat stirring constantly. Remove from the flame and add the vanilla. Pour through a strainer into a baking dish. Put the dish into a roasting pan and surround it with an inch or so of boiling water. Bake it in a preheated oven at 300° for 25 minutes or until the custard is just setting around the edges but is still soft in the middle. Remove from the oven and let it sit in the waterbath while it cools. Then refrigerate the custard for at least two hours or overnight. Just before serving sprinkle the custard with the brown sugar and put under a very hot broiler for a few seconds. If you cannot get your broiler hot enough, put the dish in cracked ice so the custard won't overcook while the brown sugar forms a nice hard crust. Serve immediately or chill again and serve.

Grouse Pancetta
Julienned Celery and Zucchini
Fried Polenta
Poached Prunes and Apricots with Cognac and Cream

Serves four

If you are unfamiliar with pancetta I recommend it most highly. It is essentially Italian-cured bacon and ranges in quality depending where you buy it. It can be bought in almost any supermarket delicatessen or Italian market.

Polenta is a starch and an excellent alternative to the ones you get so tired of serving. A form of polenta was used as a staple by the Roman soldiers when they fought against Hannibal, which says nothing about its taste but does date its use. Listed in almost all the general cookbooks (*Joy of Cooking, New York Times Cookbook*) I find it interesting that it seems never to get served. So try it, you will like it.

GROUSE PANCETTA

4 grouse
   Pancetta (approximately 1 lb.)
   Fresh sage leaves
1 garlic clove, peeled
   Salt and pepper

Dice about half the pancetta into ⅛-inch pieces. Crush the garlic and add it to the pancetta along with a few sage leaves and salt and pepper to taste. Stuff each bird with the mixture and truss. Cover with sage leaves and then whole slices of pancetta. Wrap each bird in foil or preferably in the cooking type of brown paper bag painted with oil. Roast at 350° for 40 minutes. Open it up at the table, the aroma is splendid!

JULIENNED CELERY AND ZUCCHINI

6 stalks celery
1 zucchini
2 tbsp. unsalted butter
Salt and pepper

Scrape the outside of each celery stalk (except for the young tender ones) with a vegetable peeler and cut into 2-inch lengths. Now julienne into ⅛-inch sticks. Cut the zucchini into 2-inch chunks and then julienne into ⅛ inch sticks. Saute the celery and zucchini together in butter till they are hot but still crisp. Season with salt and pepper.

FRIED POLENTA

1 cup cornmeal
½ cup (1 stick) unsalted butter
1 cup water
3 cups milk
½ tsp. nutmeg
Fat to fry in (bacon, pancetta or butter)
1 onion
Salt and pepper

Chop the onion very fine and sauté it in the butter till translucent. Add the milk and bring it to a boil. Combine the cornmeal and water, stir with a fork, and then add it to the boiling milk and onion mixture. Stir continuously until the mixture is so thick the spoon stands up in it. Remove it from the heat and add the nutmeg and season with salt and pepper. Grease a cookie sheet and spread the polenta ½ to ¼-inch thick on it. Let stand until cool and slightly hardened. Now cut with cookie cutters and fry the shapes in the fat till they are brown. Serve.

POACHED PRUNES AND APRICOTS WITH COGNAC AND CREAM

    1   bottle of good white wine
    12 orange rind slivers
    12 lemon rind slivers
    ½   lb. pitted and dried
        prunes
    ½   lb. dried apricots
    1   cup cream
    ⅛   cup cognac or armagnac
        Several cloves

Shave an orange and a lemon with a potato peeler making sure not to get any white part of the rind. Put 12 of the shavings from the orange and 12 from the lemon into a pan with the wine and cloves. Bring the mixture to a boil and let simmer for a few minutes. Add the prunes and apricots and let sit for 48 hours or more.

When ready to serve, whip the cream with the cognac in it and serve on top of the fruit.

**Spitted Woodcock
Green Beans with Wild Mushrooms
Baked Goat Cheese
Peach and Pear Ice with Crystallized Violets**

Serves four

The grape leaves are found in most supermarkets or can be left out of this recipe entirely if you can't get any.

Don't feel that you must instantly become a wild mushroom expert and run into the woods with your basket in order to follow this menu. True wild mushroom experts are hard to come by. I don't know if this is because fool-proof wild mushroom identification is so hard it requires an I.Q. level not common to most of us or because wild mushroom "experts" die young. But most of us who eat wild mushrooms seem to have two methods of obtaining them: Learn one or possibly two types of absolutely distinct, non-harmful mushrooms, like puff balls or chicken-of-the-woods, and never pick anything else. Or, buy them dried which you can do more and more easily as people tire of the bland taste from the cultivated mushrooms.

SPITTED WOODCOCK

8	woodcock
8	bacon strips
8	grape leaves
	French bread slices (10 or so depending on the way the birds are spitted).
4	tbsp. armagnac or cognac
1⅓	cups stock
4	oz. unsalted butter (1 stick) at room temperature and cut into bits
	Salt and pepper

Truss each bird and wrap first in a strip of bacon and then in a grape leaf. Spit the birds placing a buttered piece of French bread on either side of each bird. Lay the skewered birds and bread in a roasting pan and cook in the oven at 450° for 20 minutes. After cooking, place the birds and bread on heated plates. In the roasting pan add the cognac. Scraping the bottom of the pan with a wire whisk add the stock and, over a high flame, cook until the liquid is reduced to about ¾ cup. Now whisk in the butter and season with salt and pepper. This is meant to be just a moistener for the birds, not a real sauce.

GREEN BEANS WITH WILD MUSHROOMS

1 lb. green beans
1 oz. dried wild mushrooms
2 tbsp. unsalted butter
Salt and pepper

Blanch the green beans and then chill them immediately in ice water. Reconstitute the mushrooms in a little warm water. Rinse the mushrooms in cool water saving the reconstituted juice. Reduce the juice in a sauté pan (be sure not to get any of the mushrooms' grit in the pan) until it is just a glaze on the bottom of the pan. Melt the butter with the glaze and add the mushrooms and beans. Sauté, then season with salt and pepper.

BAKED GOAT CHEESE

4 ½-inch slices of goat cheese
   (or an amount that looks
   appropriate for four
   individual servings)
½ cup olive oil
   Sprig of fresh thyme
1 tsp. dried thyme
⅔ cup fine-sifted bread
   crumbs
   Lettuce leaves (Bibb or
   Boston mixed with
   bittergreens are good)
   tossed with a tasty
   vinaigrette

Marinate the slices of cheese in the olive oil and thyme sprig for a day or more.

Mix the bread crumbs with the dried thyme and dredge the slices of marinated cheese in the dry mixture making sure to cover the slices well.

Bake in a preheated oven at 400° for about 5 minutes till the cheese just starts to bubble. Place the lettuce on individual salad plates and, with a spatula, lay the cheese on top. Serve immediately.

PEACH AND PEAR ICE WITH CRYSTALLIZED VIOLETS

2	lbs. ripe peaches
2	lbs. ripe pears
1½	Twelve-ounce jars of peach jam
1½	Twelve-ounce jars of pear jam
	Pinch of salt
	Lemon juice to taste

Make cach ice separately. Heat the peach jam slowly till it has melted. Skin the peaches and remove the stone. Slice the peaches and purée in a blender or food processor. Now purée together with the melted jam. Add a pinch of salt and season with lemon juice to taste. Strain into cake tins and cover with plastic wrap. Make sure the wrap is flush with the ice, then cover with foil. Freeze for several hours. Repeat the process for the pear ice. They should be served together quite soft and garnished with crystallized violets. (You can buy the crystallized violets in your gourmet shop.)

Dove Salad
Cornsticks
Tangerine Sorbet

Serves four

I know, I know. It is a terrible pain in the neck to pluck and roast these little tiny birdies, particularly as you throw out the skin later. But it is worth it. And remember—there has been some trouble and expense gone to getting them in the first place.

Walnut oil is expensive and does go rancid more readily than most cooking oils but it is a great addition to this and many recipes and worth ordering from or buying in a gourmet shop.

Sorbets and ices, I have found, are very dependent on the liqueur that is added and I think it wise, particularly with this sorbet, to try and use the Mandarin Napoleon recommended. It truly adds to the flavor.

DOVE SALAD

6	roasted dove
1	head chicory or escarole
1	head Bibb lettuce
2	tbsp. oil
½	cup walnuts
1	tbsp. vinegar
⅛	tsp. salt
	Ground pepper
¼	tsp. prepared mustard
¼	cup walnut oil
2	tbsp. unsalted butter
1	cup white wine

Wrap the dove in bacon strips, truss, and place in a small roasting pan. Pour white wine over them and cook at 400° for 20 minutes. Let cool and then remove the meat from the bones. Discard the skin and chop the meat into small pieces. Now in the roasting pan where the dove cooked combine the vinegar, salt, a few pepper grinds, the mustard and the walnut oil. Whisk this together over a low flame.

Wash the chicory and Bibb lettuce. Sauté the walnuts in butter and chop. Now toss the dove, lettuce and walnuts together in a bowl with the vinegar mixture. Add salt and pepper or lemon juice to taste.

CORNSTICKS

1½ cups cornmeal
2   tsp. baking powder
1   tsp. salt
¼   cup flour
2   tbsp. sugar
2   eggs
1   cup buttermilk
3   tbsp. bacon drippings

Sift together the cornmeal, baking powder, salt, and flour. Beat the eggs, then add the buttermilk and bacon drippings and combine with the dry ingredients. Bake in a 425° oven for 15 to 25 minutes (depends on whether you cook them in cornstick molds or muffin tins).

TANGERINE SORBET

10–12 tangerines
1   cup sugar
      Pinch of salt
1   tbsp. Mandarin Napoleon
      liqueur (tangerine liqueur)
      Splash of lemon juice
      (Remember to have enough
      ice and salt for your ice
      cream freezer, too).

Squeeze enough tangerines so you have 1 quart of juice. Boil ½ a cup of water and add the sugar and cook for 5 minutes. Let cool. Add the sugar syrup to the fruit juice as needed to please your taste. Add the salt and lemon juice to help the taste and then pour in the liqueur. Chill the mixture in the canister from your ice cream maker. Then freeze according to the ice cream machine's directions.

Fried Dove
Zucchini with Tomato
Gorganzola Polenta
Toll House Cookies

Serves four

In a cookbook I was reading once, polenta was described as "hardtack." Perhaps because plain polenta, like most starches, has a blandness similar to the hard biscuits used by soldiers. Polenta's taste depends strongly on how it is cooked and what can be added to its taste. This, of course, is one of the great virtues of any starch; particularly so with polenta. Cheese is a great addition to polenta.

Toll House cookies seem a little silly to put into a cookbook. But clearly they are a most favorite cookie and should be baked more often. In this one exception to my rule of always using unsalted butter, I think chocolate chip cookies come out better using salted butter.

FRIED DOVE

10   dove, breasted out
½   cup (1 stick) clarified unsalted butter
1½   cups fine bread crumbs (strained)
¼   tsp. dried thyme
½   cup flour
2   eggs
2   tsp. oil
2   tsp. water
    Salt and pepper

Combine the flour, thyme and a dash of salt and pepper. Combine the eggs, oil and water and mix well. Dip the breasts first in the flour mixture, then in the egg mixture and finally in the crumbs, making sure to thoroughly coat the breasts with each dip. The breasts can rest on a cake rack for 20 minutes or so. Heat enough clarified butter over a medium flame to cover the pan bottom by ⅛ inch. Cook the breasts 3–4 minutes per side till they are lightly brown and done to the touch.

ZUCCHINI WITH TOMATO

6 small zucchini
4 small tomatoes
  Unsalted butter
  Basil
  Salt and
  pepper

Make four deep cuts into each zucchini, slicing almost to the base and creating a fan out of each zucchini. Slice the tomatoes and slip them into the zucchini cuts. Arrange carefully in a buttered baking dish and sprinkle with basil. Dot with butter and bake in a 350° oven for 20 minutes or until tender. Place in a serving dish with a spatula and season wih salt and pepper.

GORGANZOLA POLENTA

¾ cup cornmeal
1 small onion chopped fine
  (optional)
2 cups milk
6 tbsp. unsalted butter
½ cup heavy cream
5 oz. gorganzola, diced
½ tsp. nutmeg
2–3 tsp. kosher salt
  Pepper

If you are using the onion, sauté it in the butter until translucent. Then, in a small saucepan, bring the onion, butter and milk to a boil. Add the cornmeal slowly, stirring constantly till thick and the spoon can stand up in it. Be careful as the polenta will spit at you. Remove from the heat and add the cheese, nutmeg, salt, cream and pepper and mix well. Turn immediately into buttered muffin tins and let rest till set. Remove from the tin and put in a heavy oven-proof pan and cook at 400° for 15 minutes (if you like, you can add a little more cheese to the tops of the polenta muffins before putting them in the oven.)

Preserved Woodcock with Olives
Basil Pasta
Sun-dried Tomato Bread
Cantaloupe Ice

Serves four

The concept of cooking and eating an undrawn bird comes from Europe where it is quite common and anyone who has spent time there can't understand having a game cookbook without recipes for birds in the round. This, however, does not mean you have to try it. I have not, although my husband has and says it is quite good.

Sun-dried tomatoes, listed in the next recipe, are no longer very difficult to find. Most often found in Italian grocery stores or in gourmet shops in canisters like any other dried fruit, they also are available packed in oil at a higher cost. They are wonderful and worth whatever price you are asked to pay. If you cannot find them, this recipe will work without them.

The cantaloupe ice is very dependent on using a ripe, maybe even an over-ripe cantaloupe. It is not worth the trouble without one and raspberry or peach should be substituted.

PRESERVED WOODCOCK WITH OLIVES

4	woodcock	½	tsp. rosemary
8	oz. black, pitted Nicoise olives	2	large sprigs (or 3 tsp. dried) of thyme
8	oz. salt pork, cut into sticks 1 inch by ¼ inch	20	peppercorns
4	garlic cloves, peeled and crushed	5	tbsp. olive oil
8	juniper berries	3	tbsp. cognac
			Salt and pepper

Pluck the woodcock and leave them in the round (undrawn).

In a saucepan put the olives, salt pork and 1 quart water. Bring the water to a boil and then simmer for 5 minutes. Drain in a strainer and then rinse the olives in cold water.

In a tureen arrange the woodcock and sprinkle them with salt and pepper, the crushed garlic, thyme, rosemary, peppercorns, juniper berries, and the olive/salt pork combination. Combine the olive oil, cognac and a little water and paint each bird with it. Cover the tureen with a tight-fitting lid and cook in a preheated oven at 250° for 4 hours. The meat should be so soft it could be spread.

BASIL PASTA

1 lb. pasta
1 large bunch fresh basil
⅓ cup vinegar
Touch of lemon juice
1 cup olive oil
1 tbsp. prepared mustard
2 large cloves garlic
6 oz. goat cheese
Salt and pepper
Hot pepper flakes
1 bay leaf

In the cup of olive oil cook the peeled garlic cloves over a medium-low heat for about 20 minutes or until the garlic is soft but still holds its shape. Add the bay leaf while it is still hot and let sit overnight.

Make a little vinaigrette with the vinegar, lemon juice, mustard and salt and pepper. Pour the vinaigrette into a blender and add the basil with the stems removed and the olive oil garlic (less the bay leaf). Blend till smooth. Check for seasoning.

Cook the pasta particularly *al dente* (it will absorb the moisture from the basil mixture and become mushy if cooked till soft). Drain the pasta, cool a little (or it will discolor the basil vinaigrette and make its brilliant green appearance not so attractive) and toss with the basil vinaigrette. Sprinkle with red pepper flakes and crumbled goat cheese. Decorate with any extra little basil leaves.

SUN-DRIED TOMATO BREAD

3 cups all-purpose flour
1 pkg. dry yeast
½ cup sun-dried
  tomatoes
⅓ cup pitted black olives
1 tsp. salt
¼ cup wine
¼ cup olive oil
A sprig of thyme
2 cloves of garlic

In a medium size bowl mix 1 cup of the flour with the yeast and add enough warm water (not hot water) to make a wet spongy ball. Try not to work the ball too much when forming it. Fill the bowl with warm water so the ball is on the bottom. Let sit 5 to 15 minutes until the ball pops to the surface. Meanwhile take the remaining amount of flour (this can be all white flour or a mixture such as ⅔ white and ⅓ whole wheat) and put it on top of the counter. Make a trench in the middle of the pile and add the salt. Reconstitute the tomatoes by cooking them in the oil, wine, thyme, and garlic over a medium-low heat until they are soft. Let them cool and then chop them coarsely. Add the olives, the reconstituted tomatoes and some of the oil and wine mixture to the flour trench. You may also need to add a couple tablespoons of water, too. Fluff the flour with your fingers so the other ingredients get worked through. The mixture should be slightly cohesive but not wet, as the yeast/flour ball will be quite wet. When the ball has risen to the surface of the water, scoop it out and set in the middle of your pile of flour. Knead the ball and the flour together and continue to knead for 8 minutes or so. Put the dough in a buttered bowl with a towel over it and place in a warm spot to rise two hours. Punch down and let rise again or shape and bake in a preheated oven at 425° till done (about 35–40 minutes). Remember it can rise and be punched down four times, after that the yeast dies. Also, after the first rising it can be punched down and left to rise slowly overnight in the refrigerator.

CANTALOUPE ICE

2   very ripe cantaloupes
¾ cup confectioners' sugar
     Lemon juice to taste
     A pinch of salt
1   tbsp. white rum
     (Make sure you have enough ice
     and salt for your ice cream
     machine)

Halve the cantaloupes and scoop out the seeds. Now scoop out the fruit and make sure you have about 1 quart. Purée the cantaloupe in a blender and then add the sugar, salt, and lemon juice sparingly until the mixture tastes right. Now add the rum and make any adjustments for taste. Place the cantaloupe mixture in the canister of your ice cream machine and place in the refrigerator for a couple of hours. Then freeze it in the machine according to the manufacturer's directions. For a nice effect you can pack the ice cream back into the cantaloupe shells.

Minted Dove
Leg of Lamb
White Bean Puree
Green Salad
Stuffed Oranges

Serves four

Mint saves the reputation of many a black-thumbed gardener and chances are if you have a source you have an abundant source. So use it lavishly in this recipe.

We've recommended soaking the white beans for only an hour. That overnight business is passé and a leftover from the trading post days.

If you don't have a favorite way to cook a leg of lamb, here is a method we recommend:

Remove all the fat from a 6–8 pound leg of lamb. Stick slivers of garlic and leaves of rosemary randomly into it at an angle and brush with olive oil. Let sit in the refrigerator for 1–2 days. Cook in a preheated oven at 400° for 12 minutes per pound.

MINTED DOVE

60	mint leaves
8–10	dove, skinned, the breasts removed, and the carcasses saved
6	oz. very lean salted pork
5	tbsp. unsalted butter
2	tbsp. cognac
¼	tsp. basil reconstituted in hot water
⅛	tsp. garlic, chopped fine
2	small shallots, chopped fine
	Several peppercorns, crushed with the blade of a large knife
	Sprigs of thyme and rosemary (or dried)
1	bay leaf
1	cup wine
	Salt
	Pepper

Whip 4 tablespoons of butter until it is fluffy and soft. Add the garlic and basil and mix thoroughly. Season with salt and pepper to taste and chill. When the butter is cold enough make 32 balls with a small melon baller. They should be about the size of a peanut. Set on wax paper and freeze. Now sauté the shallots in 1 tablespoon of butter for a few seconds. Cover and wilt but do not let brown. Grind the dove breasts in a food processor and mix together with the shallot and the cognac. Salt and pepper to taste. Sauté a tiny amount of the meat mixture to check for seasoning.

Remove the frozen balls of compound butter from the freezer. Dip your fingers in cognac and cover butter ball with several tablespoons of the dove mixture and then wrap with 1 or 2 mint leaves. Set the wrapped dove on a steamer rack in the refrigerator. Cut or crush up the dove carcasses. Brown in the oven and set in the bottom of the steamer. Cover the carcasses with wine and water and bring to a boil. Add the bay leaf and sprigs of rosemary and thyme. Reduce to a simmer and cook for 30 minutes to make a fragrant broth. Now place the rack with the mint/dove bundles on it into the steamer making sure the rack does not touch the broth. Cover tightly with a lid and steam gently for 5 minutes. Serve as an *hors d'ouevre* or a first course.

WHITE BEAN PURÉE

1	lb. white beans, soaked an hour
2½	cups chicken stock
2½	cups water
1	onion
2	cloves
1	bay leaf
	Pinch of thyme
	A few parsley stems
	Salt and pepper
¾	cup heavy cream
½	cup (1 stick) unsalted butter, softened

Drain the soaking beans and pour in the water and broth (if you don't have any chicken stock, all water and 2 chicken boullion cubes is fine). Peel the onion and push the cloves into it. Add the the onion, bay leaf, thyme, parsley stems and salt and pepper to the bean pot and bring to a boil. Simmer until the beans are tender (about ½ to 1 hour). **Remove bay leaf.** In small batches, churn up the bean mixture in a food processor, zipping it for 1 second so as not to **purée** but just to break the skins of the beans. Push through a strainer back into the pot and mix in the butter and cream. Reheat gently and season with salt and pepper.

STUFFED ORANGES

4 large navel oranges
1 qt. orange ice or sherbet
Sprigs of mint

Cut off the top of each orange and pith and scoop out the orange inside. Rinse and let drain. Soften the sherbet or ice and then fill each orange shell. Refreeze and then decorate with sprigs of mint.

Quail Soup
Pasta with Chestnuts and Pignolis
Olive Oil and Salt Bread
Custard Oranges

Serves four

The olive oil and salt bread will be a flop if you don't use a good green olive oil and the kosher salt. Also, making the ¼ inch holes is difficult and the utmost care should be taken. It is terrific bread and worth the trouble.

Whenever you make a custard dessert, flavoring (as in this case the Cointreau) is essential. If the liqueur cabinet cannot provide it, vanilla is a good substitute.

QUAIL SOUP

10 quail, skinned	2–3 juniper berries
1½ qts. chicken stock	1 large carrot, chopped fine
2 cups cream	2 shallots or onions, chopped
3 tbsp. sour cream	fine
4 tbsp. rice	3 tbsp. unsalted butter
4 slices French bread cut into ½- inch cubes	Salt and pepper
	Bouquet garni

Remove the breasts from the quail and set aside. Crush and break up the remaining carcasses and brown them in the butter. Add the carrot and shallots, toss, then cover the pan and cook over a low flame for 15 minutes. Add the stock and bring to a boil. Add the bouquet garni, juniper berries and rice. Reduce the flame and simmer for 2 hours.

Cube the French bread and fry. Set aside.

Slice the quail breasts on the diagonal and sauté quickly (about 30 seconds) in sizzling butter. Set aside.

Bring cream to a boil and reduce to simmer. Stir every now and then until it is halved in quantity and thickens. Set aside.

Once the carcasses have simmered for two hours remove and, along with the vegetables, grind up in a food processor or meat grinder. Then grind again in a blender. Push the purée through a stainer, scraping the bottom, and then return it to the broth discarding the bones, etc. Bring it to a boil and stir in the reduced cream. Check taste for salt and pepper. Remove from the heat and blend in the sour cream. Add the pieces of breast meat and the croutons just before serving.

91

PASTA WITH CHESTNUTS AND PIGNOLIS

½ lb. prepared pasta
1 cup heavy cream
¼ cup pignolis
½ lb. chestnuts
4 tbsp. unsalted butter
Salt and pepper
1 tsp. sage

Roast the chestnuts under the broiler till their shells are slightly black and cracked. Let them cool then peel and slice them so you have about ½ cup of chestnuts. Sauté the pignolis in butter till light brown then add the chestnuts and sauté a bit more. Reduce the cream by letting it boil slowly in a frying pan till it is halved in quantity then add the sage. Cook the pasta, drain and wash, and return it to the cooking pan and toss with the cream. Add the pignolis and chestnuts and check for seasoning.

OLIVE OIL AND SALT BREAD

3 cups all-purpose flour
1 pkg. dry yeast
2 tbsp. thyme
1 tsp. salt
1 tbsp. kosher salt
¼ cup good green olive oil

In a medium size bowl mix 1 cup of the flour with the yeast and add enough warm water (not hot water) to make a moist and cohesive ball. Try not to work the ball too much when forming it. Fill the bowl with warm water so the ball is on the bottom. Let sit 5 to 15 minutes until the ball pops to the surface. Meanwhile take the remaining amount of flour (this can be all white flour or a mixture such as ⅔ white and ⅓ whole wheat) and put it on top of the counter. Make a trench in the middle of the pile and add the salt. Reconstitute the thyme by pouring a little hot water in with it first and then add it to the flour trench. You may also need to add a couple tablespoons of water, too. Fluff the flour with your fingers so the other ingredients get worked through. The mixture should be slightly cohesive but not wet as the yeast/flour ball will be quite wet. When the ball has risen to the surface of the water, scoop it out and set in the middle of your pile of flour. Knead the ball and the flour together and continue to knead for 8 minutes or so. Put the dough in a buttered bowl with a towel over it and place in a warm spot and let rise two hours. Punch down and shape into a round, flat pancake about 8–12 inches wide. Let rise again and very carefully poke ¼-inch holes all around the top of the bread with the end of a wooden spoon. Fill the holes with the olive oil (or you can use walnut oil) and sprinkle with the kosher salt. Bake in a preheated oven at 425° till done (about 35–40 minutes). Remember it can rise and be punched down four times, after that the yeast dies. Also, after the first rising it can be punched down and left to rise slowly overnight in the refrigerator.

CUSTARD ORANGES

3   egg yolks
⅓   cup sugar
1⅓ cups heavy cream
1½ oz. Cointreau
4   large navel oranges
    Cocoa Powder

Cut off the top of each orange and scoop out the inside. Rinse and let drain. Beat the egg yolks and sugar together then add the Cointreau. Now whip one cup of the cream until it is stiff. Mix in ⅓ of the whipped cream and then fold in the remaining cream. Fill each orange with the egg-cream mixture and set on a plate in the refrigerator for at least two hours. When ready to serve whip the remaining ⅓ cup cream and put a dollop on each orange top. Dust with cocoa.

Pheasant Sandwich
Ruffed Grouse Sandwich with Hazelnut Butter
Cold Wild Rice Salad
Assorted Cheeses (Brie, Goat, Saga)
Olives
Fresh Fruit
Cookies and Cheese

Serves four

Ruffed grouse are my favorite upland bird to eat. Unfortunately, they have also proven to be nearly impossible for me to shoot; making them into sandwich meat is almost more than I could bear. Fortunately, I've had the pleasure of hunting with the most charming and successful of grouse hunters, Richard Montague. Mr. Montague not only makes his own beer, speaks several dead languages, has owned a series of well-mannered Brittanies and a pretty, little bicycle shop in remote Vershire, Vermont, but he manages to fill his freezer with 30 to 40 grouse each season. It is to characters such as Richard that this recipe is dedicated.

For some reason the upland birds are more difficult to pluck than the water fowl. The skin tears more readily and, particularly in the case of pheasant, the feathers are more difficult to pull out. Consequently, I suggest using this recipe on leftover pheasant so you get two meals for the work of one plucking. Another alternative to plucking for sandwich meat is to save this recipe for the times the hunter visits his happy pheasant preserve. Most private pheasant preserve owners ask their hunters if they would prefer to take home the specific birds shot that day or ones already plucked and cleaned. Certainly for a sandwich-meat bird pride of ownership can be foregone.

PHEASANT SANDWICH

  Leftover pheasant or roast
  pheasant sliced thin
½ tbsp. basil
1 cup (2 sticks) unsalted butter
1 finely chopped shallot
¼ tsp. grated lemon rind
  Watercress
  Salt and pepper

Whip the butter until it is fluffy. Reconstitute the basil in a little hot water and add it to the butter along with the shallot and lemon rind. Spread French bread thickly with the compound butter and lay on the pheasant and watercress.

RUFFED GROUSE SANDWICH WITH HAZELNUT BUTTER

2 grouse, roasted and cooled
½ cup hazelnuts
1 cup (2 sticks) unsalted butter
1 tbsp. finely chopped parsley
Salt and pepper

Toast the hazelnuts on a cookie sheet in the oven till they are brown. Be careful not to burn them. Remove the nuts from the oven and cover with a tea towel for 15 minutes or so to create steam, then rub off the skins with the tea towel. Chop finely. Whip the butter and add the nuts, chopped parsley, salt and pepper to taste. Spread whole wheat bread thickly with the compound butter and lay thin slices of grouse on top.

COLD WILD RICE SALAD

½ cup wild rice
1 cup green seedless grapes
4–5 radishes
2 tbsp. vinegar
½ cup olive oil
1 tsp. prepared mustard
1 shallot, chopped
1 tsp. tarragon

Place the rice in a pot with 3 inches of water covering it. Bring to a boil and then turn the heat down and let simmer, uncovered, until all the water is gone (about 30 minutes). Slice the radishes very thin. Cut the grapes in half. Toss the radishes and grapes in with the rice. Combine the remaining ingredients in the blender and zip on high for a few seconds. Check for seasoning. Pour the vinaigrette over the rice mixture and check again for seasoning.

Roast Wild Turkey
Fontina Polenta
Fava Beans, Peas and Pancetta
Green Salad
Rhubarb Tart

Serves four

Although many states now offer a fall turkey hunt this menu is specifically designed for a spring turkey hunt. Both rhubarb and the fava beans are not available fresh except in the spring.

ROAST WILD TURKEY

1   wild turkey
½   cup (1 stick) unsalted butter
1   tbsp. dried thyme
     Sprigs of fresh thyme
     Salt and pepper
10 or so bacon strips

Make a compound butter by whipping the unsalted butter. Reconstitute the dried thyme by soaking it in a little hot water and then add it in to the butter. Whip the butter and add salt, pepper, and lemon juice to taste. Refrigerate for 1 hour or overnight. Spread the butter between the skin of the turkey and the meat trying not to tear the skin. Salt and pepper the cavity and stuff with the sprigs of fresh thyme. Truss the turkey and lay the bacon strips over it. Soak a covering of cheese cloth in butter and cover the whole bird with it. Roast at 325° for 10 minutes per pound. Baste the turkey with its own juices every ½ hour. If the bird has not browned nicely ½ hour before he is supposed to be done, remove the cheese cloth.

FONTINA POLENTA

¾ cup·cornmeal
1 small onion
(optional)
2 cups milk
6 tbsp. unsalted butter
½ cup heavy cream
5 oz. fontina, diced
½ tsp. nutmeg
2–3 tsp. kosher salt
Pepper

If you are using the onion, sauté it in the butter until translucent. Then, in a small saucepan bring the onion, butter and milk to a boil. Add the cornmeal slowly, stirring constantly till thick and the spoon can stand up in it. Be careful as the polenta will spit at you. Now add the cheese, nutmeg and salt. Remove from the heat and beat in the cream and pepper. Turn immediately into buttered muffin tins and let rest till set. Remove from the tin and put in a heavy oven-proof pan and cook at 400° for 15 minutes (if you like, you can add a little more cheese to the tops of the polenta muffins before putting them in the oven.)

FAVA BEANS, PEAS, AND PANCETTA

4 oz. pancetta
1 box frozen peas, defrosted
(Birdseye's Tender Tiny Peas
are better than most fresh unless
from your own garden)
1 lb. fava beans

Remove the fava beans from their pods. Peel the outer skin from each bean. This is very tedious and boring but important and worth doing. Steam the beans till barely done, about 5 minutes. Then **dip** in ice water. Dice the pancetta into ⅛-inch pieces and sauté over a low heat until it is not quite crispy. Remove it from the pan. Rinse the defrosted peas in cool water and drain well. Put the peas and the fava beans into the pan with the pancetta fat and, over a medium flame, heat through. Put into a serving dish, add salt, pepper, pancetta and a little butter and toss.

RHUBARB TART

3 lbs. rhubarb (preferably the
  young sticks)
¾ cup sugar
1 lemon, grated
  Splash of vanilla or sherry
⅔ cup crème fraîche or a mixture of
  sour cream and heavy cream
2 tbsp. confectioners' sugar
½ tsp. powdered cloves
½ lb. pastry

Roll out the pastry into a buttered 9-inch tart or pastry dish and refrigerate for 1 hour.

With a knife peel the thin outer layer from each stick of rhubarb and slice very thinly. Put in a heavy saucepan with the granulated sugar. Cover and cook 15 minutes over a medium low heat. Then remove the lid and turn the heat up to evaporate all the juices. Stir constantly so it will not stick and burn. Once it has reached the consistency of jam remove and let cool. Add the lemon rind and a few drops of the vanilla or sherry.

Prick the bottom of the refrigerated pastry shell with a fork and place foil tightly over the pastry. Fill with pie weights or beans and cook on the lower shelf of a preheated oven at 425° for 8 minutes. Remove the foil and weights, prick the crust again, sprinkle with a little granulated sugar and return it to the oven for 5 more minutes or until the crust is caramelized and golden. Remove it from the oven and carefully slide the crust onto a cake rack to cool.

Whip the cream and sour cream (or just the crème fraîche) together with the confectioners' sugar and clove. When it's thick, spread it over the bottom of the pastry shell. Then spread the rhubarb over the whipped cream mixture and serve within 30 minutes.

Pheasant in Wine
Fiddleheads
Baked Grits
Strawberry Tart

Serves four

Fiddleheads are spring-time ferns which have not unfolded and look like wheels on the end of a stalk. They can be collected in the woods or, I've noticed, more and more grocery stores are selling them. There is one advantage to buying the store bought ones, the chaff which we refer to in the recipe has at least been partially removed. Lest you be too cavalier with this notion I impart the following tale.

Set on always trying to obtain wild food and wanting my children to understand the bounty of the woods, the family set out on an excursion to gather fiddleheads and came home quite successfully with a large basket full. I tried everything I could think of to get the chaff off—from soaking to picking and finally in desperation I called my friends, the Renesons, who I knew to be fanciers of the vegetable. Unfortunately, Chet answered the phone. When I queried him as to how to get the moldy stuff off the fiddleheads he suggested the following: In the bow of your Grand Laker canoe place your spouse and the basket of fiddleheads. In the stern, seated at the throttle of the 50-horse Johnson, place yourself dressed in black sou'wester and hat. Once untied from the dock, speed boat at full throttle the length of a 10 mile lake with spouse holding up each individual fiddlehead and you dodging the flying chaff which is, hopefully, flying back at you.

Besides finding this method impractical from my city dwelling, Chet's deadpan delivery of the method did not convince me of reliability. However, in the years that have ensued I have been more and more tempted to try. The chaff is very, very difficult to get off and I suggest leaving all but the cleanest of fiddleheads (collected early in the day and early in the spring) to cover the forest floor.

PHEASANT IN WINE

2 pheasants, cut up
1 carrot
1 onion
½ celery stalk
1 cup chicken stock
1 cup white wine
4 tbsp. unsalted butter
 Bacon fat
3 tsp. basil
1½ tsp. cornstarch ·

First brown the pheasant pieces in a little bacon fat. Remove the pheasant from the pan. Dice the carrot, onion, and ½ celery stick into ⅛-inch dice and sauté them in the pan with the butter. Return all the pheasant pieces but the breasts to the pan, set on top of the vegetables. Add the wine and stock so the pieces are not quite covered. Bring to a simmer and add the basil. Press aluminum foil down on top of the birds so that there is no space between the liquid and the foil and then cover the pan with a lid. Cook about 20 minutes. Add the breasts and cook for an additional 5 minutes.

Put the pheasant pieces onto a warmed platter. Thicken the juices with cornstarch and pour the sauce over the birds just before serving.

FIDDLEHEADS

1 lb. fiddleheads
3 tbsp. unsalted butter
 Salt and pepper

Cut the bottoms off the fiddleheads leaving about ¾ of the stem. In a *large* soup pot or bowl full of cold water soak the fiddleheads for 5 minutes or so. Then, by the handful, rinse the fiddleheads under the faucet. Pour out the potful of water and repeat the process two or three more times or until the brown chaff has been completely removed. It is very important to remove as much of the chaff as possible because it causes the fiddleheads to be bitter. Bring a quart of salted water to boil and drop in just a handful of the fiddleheads. Cook for 3–4 minutes or until they're just tender. Scoop them out and plunge them into ice water to stop the cooking. Drain the fiddleheads and dry them on an old towel. Repeat this until you have cooked all the fiddleheads, changing the boiling water with each handful of fiddleheads. Finally sauté the fiddleheads quickly in the unsalted butter and serve. It's worth it.

BAKED GRITS

¾   cup grits
3   cups boiling water
1½ tsp. salt
2   eggs
4   tbsp. unsalted butter, sliced
      into thin pats
⅛   tsp. cayenne
½   lb. grated sharp cheddar cheese

Add the salt and grits to the boiling water and cook until done or the consistency of bubbling oatmeal. Remove from the heat and let cool slightly then add the eggs, cayenne, and cheese. Check the seasoning and then place in a buttered baking dish and cook in a preheated oven at 350° for 1 hour.

STRAWBERRY TART

1   sheet Pepperidge Farm Puff
      Pastry or your own
1   tbsp. butter
2   tbsp. sugar
2   pints strawberries
½   pint heavy cream
2   tbsp. currant jam
½   tbsp. Grand Marnier
3   tbsp. sour cream

Preheat the oven at 425° for at least 20 minutes.

Roll out the pastry and fit into a porcelain tart or quiche dish heavily buttered. Roll the rolling pin over the top to cut the extra pastry off the edges. Let rest in the refrigerator for 1 hour. Prick the pastry with a fork and then flatten a piece of foil over it. Put beans, peas, or pastry weights on top of the foil. Cook in the lower part of the hot oven for 7 minutes, then carefully open the oven and remove the foil and weights. Sprinkle with sugar and continue cooking for at least 5 minutes until the crust is a light brown with a shiny, caramelized surface. Then remove from the oven and let cool 1 minute. Slide the pastry out of the dish onto a cake rack to cool completely. Whip the cream. About half way through whipping add the Grand Marnier (Framboise is good, too) and the sour cream. Spread over the bottom of the pastry shell. Arrange the strawberries on top of the cream attractively (raspberries, blueberries or any fruit are good also). Melt the currant jam over a low flame. Remove and let cool slightly. Add a dash of the liqueur you used in the cream to the jam. Now, with a 2-inch pastry brush, paint the strawberries with the jam mixture. Serve immediately as it will become soggy if you try to hold it more than one hour.

Grilled Quail
Grilled Mushrooms
Purée of Peas
Pear Cake

Serves four

Peas are one of the few vegetables that are just as good from a frozen package as fresh. Unless you have grown them yourself and picked them yourself and they are young and tiny, then, of course, there is no comparison. But then you shouldn't be wasting them on a purée like this recipe, either.

GRILLED QUAIL

4	quail, butterflied (see page 211)
12	crushed juniper berries
4	cloves garlic, peeled and crushed
4	shallots, peeled and crushed
2	bay leaves
1	cup white wine
¼	lb. pancetta
1	tbsp. unsalted butter
2	tbsp. oil
	Salt and pepper

Dice the pancetta and sauté. When it is about half way cooked add the juniper berries, garlic cloves, shallots, bay leaves and wine. Stir together and then pour over the quail. Cover and refrigerate overnight turning the birds two or three times. Remove from the refrigerator about 1 hour before cooking.

Grill the birds in a little oil and butter bone side first as always. Cook about 3 minutes per side and baste with the marinade.

GRILLED MUSHROOMS

1	lb. large mushrooms (whole or halved)
3	tbsp. unsalted butter
	Salt and pepper

Grill the mushrooms for 3–4 minutes and then sauté them in the butter. Season with salt and pepper.

PURÉE OF PEAS

2   1-lb. bags of frozen peas
4   tbsp. unsalted butter, cut into
    pats
½   cup cream

Cook the peas in 2 cups of water, covered, till they are tender, about 10 minutes. Drain the peas and push through a strainer. Discard the skins and return the purée to the pan with the butter and cream. Whisk over a low flame for a few seconds until warm. Add salt and pepper to taste.

PEAR CAKE

2   eggs
¼   cup milk
2   tsp. vanilla, pear liqueur or
    rum
1   cup sugar
    Pinch of salt
1½ cups flour
    Rind of one orange, grated
2   lbs. fresh pears
    Butter to grease the cake pan
½   cup unflavored bread crumbs

Preheat the oven to 350°. Beat the eggs, milk and vanilla (or liqueur) together in a bowl. Add the sugar, salt and orange rind and continue beating. Now blend in the flour. Peel the pears and cut them in half. Scoop out the seeds and core and slice into pieces no more than 1 inch thick and add to the flour, egg, and sugar mixture. Grease a 9-inch cake pan with butter and then sprinkle the bread crumbs into it. Shake the crumbs all about and then empty the pan of any excess crumbs. Pour the batter into the cake tin and level it with a spoon. Bake in the preheated oven for 45 minutes or until it is a light brown. Let it cool and then remove it from the pan. The pear cake can be eaten lukewarm or cold. It's good served with a lightly whipped cream, too.

Quick Charcoal Quail
Sautéed Watercress
Cauliflower and Mayonnaise
Chocolate Cake

Serves four

Sautéed watercress is wonderful and should be used often.

Using homemade mayonnaise really makes a tremendous difference to the cauliflower and using fancy chocolate versus Baker's less of a difference to the cake even though we say it does. If short on time don't drive to the gourmet shop for the chocolate; make the mayonnaise instead.

QUICK CHARCOAL QUAIL

4 quail
   Several juniper berries per bird
4 strips of bacon

Insert several juniper berries into each bird and truss. Wrap the bird in a strip of bacon and slide onto a spit. Charcoal on the grill or if the rain begins to douse the fire roast in the oven at 350° for 20 minutes.

SAUTÉED WATERCRESS

3   bunches of watercress
3–4 tbsp. butter
   Salt and pepper

Take each bunch of watercress and cut into 2-inch lengths (the bunches should be cut approximately into thirds). Sauté the watercress in the hot unsalted butter for a second or two then add the lid for two minutes. Remove the lid and season with salt and pepper and a little more butter and serve.

CAULIFLOWER WITH MAYONNAISE

1 head cauliflower
1 cup thin mayonnaise (preferably
  homemade; see page 208). If not
  homemade thin with a little
  heavy cream.
½ tsp. prepared mustard
  Chives
  Salt and pepper

Take the leaves off the cauliflower and separate into florets leaving ½- to 1-inch stems on them. Bring several quarts of water to boil and drop the cauliflower in by handfuls. When the cauliflower is just tender remove from the boiling water and plunge into a iced bath. After it is cooled, drain. Season the mayonnaise with mustard, salt and pepper, and chives and pour over the cauliflower. Toss and serve.

CHOCOLATE CAKE

½ lb. (2 sticks) unsalted butter
½ lb. unsweetened chocolate (the
  better the chocolate, the better
  the cake)
1½ cups sugar
10 eggs, separated
1 tbsp. lemon juice
2 tbsp. orange liqueur
  (Cointreau)
1 tbsp. vanilla
  Pinch of salt
  Sprinkle of confectioners' sugar

Combine the butter and chocolate in a saucepan and melt them over a low flame. Add the vanilla, lemon juice and liqueur. Remove from the heat. Beat together the egg yolks and sugar until they ribbon lightly and then combine with the chocolate mixture. Beat the egg whites until they support a whole raw egg without sinking and then stir in ⅓ of the whites into the chocolate mixture. Fold in the remaining whites.

Butter and flour a 10-inch spring form pan. Cut a 10-inch round of wax paper and butter and flour that, placing it on the bottom of the spring form pan. Pour the cake batter into the pan and bake in a preheated oven of 250° for 2½ hours. Let cool completely and remove it from the pan. Sprinkle with confectioners' sugar.

Pheasant Salad
Soup in a Pumpkin
Basil Bread
Figs in Rum

Serves four

PHEASANT SALAD

2–3   pheasants
2   tbsp. butter
1   can (14 oz.) artichoke hearts
       (in brine)
1   cup heavy cream
1   tsp. basil
½   cup olive oil
1   tsp. mustard
2   tbsp. vinegar
½   garlic clove (finely chopped)
       Salt and pepper

Breast out the pheasant and oven poach them by doing the following: Quickly toss the breasts in the melted butter until they are just becoming white on the outside and then place them in a buttered baking dish. Cut a piece of wax paper to fit the top, butter it, and press it over the pheasant. Bake for 5 minutes at 450° or until the meat is just springy to the touch. Remember that all meat, but especially the high-in-protein game, continues to cook, often as much as by ⅓ more, after it has been removed from the heat. Now remove the breasts from the pan and skim off any fat in the juice and set the juice aside.

Meanwhile reduce the cream: Over a high heat bring the the cream to a boil. Reduce to a simmer. Add basil, salt and pepper and stir every now and then so it doesn't stick to the pan. Cook until it is halved in quantity and thick. Mix in the juices left over from cooking the pheasant and let cool. Slice the pheasant breasts on the diagonal.

Drain the artichoke hearts and soak them in cold water. Change the water 2–3 times to remove the metallic taste from the artichokes which they got from being in the can. Cut into quarters.

Combine the remaining ingredients in the blender for 30 seconds or so to make a vinaigrette. Mix the vinaigrette with the reduced cream and pheasant juices and pour over the artichokes and pheasant pieces. Toss and check for salt and pepper. Serve on lettuce with French bread.

SOUP IN A PUMPKIN

1	perfect little pumpkin which will fit in your oven and weighs about 6 lbs.
1	onion, chopped
	Bay leaf
	Several parsley stems
	Pinch of thyme
½	cup cream
	Croutons
	Chopped parsley
	Salt and pepper
½	cup (1 stick) unsalted butter
5	cups chicken stock

Scoop out the pumpkin. Discard the seeds and string and save the flesh. Be sure not to scoop too close to the skin. Cut the pumpkin flesh into small chunks and sauté it in the butter along with the onion until the pumpkin is soft. Add the stock, herbs, and parsley stems. Season with salt and pepper and let cook until the mixture is quite soft. **Remove bay leaf.** Purée in the blender or a food processor and then strain. Add the cream and check for seasoning. Return the pumpkin soup to the pumpkin shell and cook in the oven for 40 minutes at 350°. Garnish with the croutons and chopped parsley and serve scraping the pumpkin shell sides as you ladle the soup into the bowls.

BASIL BREAD

3 cups all-purpose flour
1 pkg. dry yeast
2 tbsp. basil
1 tsp. salt

In a medium size bowl mix 1 cup of the flour with the yeast and add enough warm water (not hot) to make a moist and cohesive ball. Fill the bowl with warm water so the ball is covered. Let sit until the ball pops to the surface, 5 to 15 minutes. Meanwhile take the remaining amount of flour (this can be all white flour or a mixture such as ⅔ white and ⅓ whole wheat) and put it on top of the counter. Make a trench in the middle of the pile and add the salt. Reconstitute the basil by pouring a little hot water in with it first and stirring then add it to the flour trench. You will need to add more water, a few tablespoons at a time, fluffing it into the flour with your fingers. The mixture should be slightly cohesive but not wet as the yeast/flour ball will be quite wet. When the ball has risen to the surface of the water, scoop it out and set in the middle of your pile of flour. Knead the ball and the flour together and continue to knead for 8 minutes or so. Put the dough in an oiled or floured bowl with a towel over it and place in a warm spot to rise two hours or until doubled in bulk. Punch down and let rise again or shape and bake in a preheated oven at 425° till done (about 35–40 minutes). Remember it can be punched down four times, after that the yeast dies. Also, after the first rising it can be punched down and left to rise slowly overnight in the refrigerator.

FIGS IN RUM

2 lbs. fresh figs
1 cup sugar
1 cup water
4 tbsp. rum
1 vanilla bean
  Pinch of thyme or a sprig of
  fresh thyme
1 cup heavy cream

Wash and drain the figs. Simmer the water and sugar together for 5 minutes then add the figs and vanilla bean. Cook slowly over a low heat for 1 hour. Remove from the heat and let cool. Add the rum and cover the fruit tightly. Let it all sit in the refrigerator for 2 days. Whip the cream and serve on top of the figs.

Pheasant and Cabbage
Cooked Apples
Cheese

Serves four

Cintra and I are very lucky to live near a wonderful apple farm which maintains some 30 or 40 different types of apple trees. The farmer lovingly lists on paper for his customers each type of apple, its unique characteristics, history, and how the apple should be used. It would be nice to refer you to a specific type of cooking apple for this recipe but impractical and very provincial. I do recommend making inquires to local grocers or orchard owners as to what are the best cooking (versus eating) apples in your area to buy.

PHEASANT AND CABBAGE

½ head of red cabbage
½ head of green cabbage
2 whole pheasants, plucked and
  ready for roasting
  Fresh herbs (or dried)
4 thin slices of pancetta
2 tbsp. unsalted butter

To prepare the pheasants, stuff the cavity of each bird with the fresh herbs and truss. Wrap each pheasant in pancetta or regular bacon and roast at 350° for 30 minutes. Remove the bacon and cook for an additional 15 or 20 minutes till the birds are brown. While the birds are cooking prepare the cabbage. Halve and then quarter each cabbage and cut off the stiff core. Slice thinly as if for cole slaw. Sauté the cabbage, each color separately, quickly in butter till cooked but still crunchy. Season with salt, pepper and a light dose of caraway. Place the birds on a warmed platter and arrange the cabbage in rings around the birds.

COOKED APPLES

4 apples
3 tbsp. unsalted butter
1 tbsp. calvados
¼ cup cream
 Salt and pepper

Make noisette butter by melting the butter over a medium-high heat in a frying pan until the butter has turned a light brown (remember it continues to darken after it is taken from the heat). Meanwhile peel and dice the apples. Cook them in the butter until just tender on a medium heat. Turn the heat to high, add the calvados and let the heat evaporate it. Pour in the cream and cook a few minutes until the cream has thickened. Season with salt and pepper.

Woodcock Armagnac
Fennel and Peas
Roast Potatoes
Garlic Toasts
Tarte Tatin

Serves four

Woodcock are perhaps my least favorite upland bird. This may be because every time I've shot one I've had such bad luck in finding the downed bird that I have a bad taste in my mouth about them before they even make it to the kitchen. More likely my distaste comes from the knowledge that they feed on worms. Ed says they are the only carnivorous upland bird; he loves them. They are many people's favorite bird and I include them here with a good shot of armagnac which makes everything all right by me.

When we do not include a specific recipe for something listed in the menu—as in this case with the roast potatoes—it is because we assume you know how to cook it and have a favorite method of doing so. Or because it requires no cooking at all.

WOODCOCK ARMAGNAC

8 woodcock
2 tbsp. hot butter
3 tbsp. armagnac
½ cup heavy cream
   Salt, pepper, lemon juice or
   mustard

Breast out the woodcock. Sauté the breasts in the hot butter very fast (about 1 minute per side) and then remove them from the pan. Add the armagnac to the juices left in the pan and stir with a wire whisk making sure to scrape the bottom. Now add the cream and cook on a high heat till thick and reduced to about half the original quantity. Season with salt and pepper and a little mustard or a few drops of lemon juice if you need more tartness. Serve over the breasts.

FENNEL AND PEAS

2 heads fennel, halved and cored
1 box frozen peas, defrosted
   (Birdseye's Tender Tiny Peas
   are the best)
2 tbsp. unsalted butter

Peel the outer stalks of the fennel with a potato peeler. Julienne all the stalks into ⅛-inch pieces cutting against the grain of the fennel. Sauté the fennel in butter for several minutes till it is tender but not limp. Now add the box of defrosted peas and heat through. Add salt and pepper to taste.

GARLIC TOASTS

1 loaf French bread
8 heads of firm garlic
5 tbsp. good green olive oil
Salt and pepper

Cut the French bread into ½-inch slices and toast on a cookie sheet in a 300° oven making sure both sides are lightly browned.

Separate all the garlic cloves, peel and remove any green sprouts. Boil all the cloves in a couple quarts of cold, salted water for 5 minutes. Drain and repeat the boiling process three more times. The garlic cloves should be easily pierced with a fork. Purée the cloves with the olive oil in a food processor or blender, or mash with a fork. Add salt and pepper to taste. Spread the garlic purée on the toast and run under the broiler to glaze. Serve.

TARTE TATIN

6 hard golden delicious apples
1 sheet Pepperidge Farm Puff
Pastry or your own
2 tbsp. butter
¾ cup sugar, plus a sprinkle
½ cup water
Sprinkle of cinnamon

Peel and slice the apples thinly. Next caramelize the sugar by cooking the water and ¾ cup sugar in a frying pan until it is light brown. Remove immediately from the heat as it will continue to cook and transfer to a cake tin. Spread the caramelized sugar over the bottom and lay the apple slices in concentric circles on top. Only the first layer will show so be sure to make that your best. Dot each layer of apples with butter and sprinkle with sugar and cinnamon. Once the pan is full roll out the pastry and cover the apples with it. Cut a few tiny holes in the pastry to let the steam escape. Cook in the middle of a preheated oven at 450° for 20 minutes. Then turn the heat down to 350° and continue to cook for 30 to 40 minutes. Remove and let cool for a few minutes and then invert onto a serving plate. If it has hardened too much, put the cake tin on a burner and remelt the caramel, then invert.

Chukar Stuffed with Hazelnuts
Grated Zucchini
Sautéed Cherry Tomatoes
Cheese, Thyme Toasts
Fresh Fruit

Serves four

CHUKAR STUFFED WITH HAZELNUTS

4   chukars, skinned
⅓ cup toasted and finely chopped
     hazelnuts
¼ cup bread crumbs, sifted fine
1   tbsp. parsley, chopped fine
2   tbsp. cream (for moistening)
     Salt and pepper
     Pinch of thyme
3   tbsp. unsalted butter

Cut the breasts off the bone. Combine the hazelnuts (Be sure to roast them in the oven, steam in a tea towel and remove skins. To chop them fine, you can use a food processor.) with the bread crumbs, 1 teaspoon of the parsley, salt and pepper, a pinch of thyme and some cream to moisten it all. Make a slice on the keel-bone edge of each breast and stuff with the nut mixture. Oven poach the breasts by doing the following: Quickly toss the breasts in 2 tablespoons of melted butter. When the breasts are just turning white remove them and put into a buttered baking dish. Cut a piece of wax paper to fit the top, butter it and press it over the chukar breasts. Bake for 5 minutes at 400° or until the meat is just springy to the touch. Slice the breast on the diagonal in three pieces and arrange attractively on a platter. Lightly brown the remaining butter in a small pan and add any juices from the poaching pan. Dribble this over the top of the breasts and sprinkle with the remaining parsley chopped fine. Season with salt and pepper.

GRATED ZUCCHINI

4 medium zucchini
2 tbsp. unsalted butter
  Salt and pepper
1 lb. spinach
1 shallot, chopped

Grate the zucchini coarsely. Put it in a strainer and sprinkle with salt. Let stand and drain for 20 minutes. Meanwhile wash the spinach, shake dry, and barely wilt it over a medium-low flame with the lid on for a second. Drain the spinach, let cool, then chop. Squeeze the water out of the zucchini. Sauté the shallot in butter over a medium heat and add the zucchini to it. Add the spinach. Stirring continuously, heat the vegetables over medium heat till hot to the touch. Add salt and pepper to taste and serve.

SAUTÉED CHERRY TOMATOES

24 cherry tomatoes
2 tbsp. unsalted butter
  Several sprigs of fresh basil (or
  any other fresh herb you may
  have; dried herbs work, too)
  Salt and pepper

Prick each cherry tomato with a pin to prevent the tomato skins from bursting and remove the green tops. Sauté in the butter till hot and sprinkle with the chopped herb and salt and pepper. Serve.

CHEESE, THYME TOAST

1 loaf French bread
½ lbs. gruyere cheese
   Sprinkles of dried thyme
   Salt
   Hot pepper flakes
¼ cup olive oil

Slice the bread and grill it. Brush each piece with oil and lay a piece of cheese on top. Sprinkle the thyme, salt and pepper flakes on top and broil till the cheese just bubbles.

Water Fowl

Most game cookbooks list duck recipes by species. We have not done that here. It took me a long time to learn that although there is tremendous difference when hunting a duck, what species he is makes very little difference once he is in the kitchen. This does not mean there is not any difference between ducks; quite the contrary. But the differences come from what his diet is, his age, what kind of weather he's been enduring, how he has been treated in the field and overall size—not specifically from what type of duck he is. In general, an older, larger duck is tougher than a young small duck. In general, a late-season duck who has already endured a time of compromising diet and hard weather will have poorer taste. And of course, whether he has been cleanly shot and carefully dressed will affect the taste. (See the chapter on "Game Care" for more details.) What a game cook needs to develop is a knowledge of how to cook the bird according to how it looks rather than how to cook him because he is a mallard or a black duck. A fleshy, pale-skinned duck with no tears in the skin and all blood and fat deposits removed properly will simply taste better.

In order to impress this fact on the reader I've removed the species names from each recipe in the hope that you will consider the condition of the duck you are about to cook first and what species he is second. The recipe should be chosen on the basis of what needs to happen to the duck more than because he is a pintail or a widgeon.

There are two broad differences that I have tried to note with each recipe. First, I've indicated when the recipe should be used for the sea ducks and second, what general size of duck the recipe calls for. The suggested sea duck recipes are based on how much you might want to cover up some of the fish taste that often goes along with their flavor. The indication on size is to give you some idea of how the temperature and allotted time were determined for cooking the duck. Any of the recipes are applicable to any species of duck—just take into account what was in mind when the recipe was being designed.

Duck with Ginger and Scallions
Sautéed Watercress
Cheese, Thyme Toast
Chocolate Cake

Serves four

DUCK WITH GINGER AND SCALLIONS

4 ducks, breasted out
1 2-inch piece of ginger root
1 bunch of scallions
1 cup stock
4 tbsp. hot unsalted butter
¼ cup sesame oil

Slice the duck breasts horizontally in half and sauté in 1 tablespoon of the butter for 3-4 minutes per side or until springy to the touch.

Chop the green part of the scallions into ¼-inch pieces. Peel and julienne the ginger into pieces 1/16 by 1 inch in size and put into a little cup with some sesame oil.

Put the cooked duck breasts onto a heated platter. Add the stock to the pan that the ducks were cooked in and cook over a high heat scraping the bottom with a wire whisk. Cook until the liquid has been reduced to ¼ cup. Whisk in the remaining 3 tablespoons of butter. Now add the ginger and scallions. Arrange the ducks attractively on the warmed platter and pour the sauce over them. Serve.

SAUTÉED WATERCRESS

3 bunches of
watercress
3-4 tbsp. unsalted butter
Salt and pepper

Take each bunch of watercress and cut into 2-inch lengths (the bunches should be cut approximately into thirds). Sauté the watercress in the hot unsalted butter for a second or two then add the lid for two minutes. Remove the lid, season with salt and pepper and a little more butter, and serve.

CHEESE, THYME TOAST

1   loaf French bread
½   lb. gruyere cheese
    Sprinkles of dried thyme
    Salt
    Hot pepper flakes
¼   cup olive oil

Slice the bread and grill it. Brush each piece with oil and lay a piece of cheese on top. Sprinkle the thyme, salt and pepper flakes on top and broil till the cheese just bubbles.

CHOCOLATE CAKE

½   lb. (2 sticks) unsalted butter
½   lb. unsweetened chocolate (the
    better the chocolate, the better
    the cake)
1½ cups sugar
10 eggs, separated
1   tbsp. lemon juice
2   tbsp. orange liqueur
    (Cointreau)
1   tbsp. vanilla
    Pinch of salt
    Sprinkle of confectioners' sugar

Combine the butter and chocolate in a saucepan and melt them over a low flame. Add the vanilla, lemon juice and liqueur. Remove from the heat. Beat together the egg yolks and sugar until they ribbon lightly and then combine with the chocolate mixture. Beat the egg whites until they support a whole raw egg without sinking and then mix in ⅓ of the whites into the chocolate mixture. Fold in the remaining whites.

Butter and flour a 10-inch spring form pan. Cut a 10-inch round of wax paper and butter and flour that, placing it on the bottom of the spring form pan. Pour the cake batter into the pan and bake in a preheated oven of 250° for 2½ hours. Let cool completely and remove it from the pan. Sprinkle with confectioners' sugar.

Ducks with Rosemary and Sage
Fontina Polenta
Zucchini Fans with Tomatoes
Coffee Ice Cream with Frangelico

Serves four

Throughout this book we recommend using fresh herbs. Often this was the type of ingredient that I secretly dreaded seeing in a recipe and either ignored by using dried instead or decided the cookbook wasn't any good. Please don't make hasty pronouncements. Cintra taught me early on that fresh herbs do make a tremendous difference, particularily when not much else is happening in the recipe. However, we do not expect you to be a gourmet cook and a green-thumb gardener. How can one body have time for both? We suggest buying little thyme plants or whatever, using them mercilessly throughout hunting season, and throwing them out when the leaves have all been used or you forget to water it. Don't worry about trying to preserve the plant for some magnificent herbal garden. Use it, throw it out, and buy more. But do use it.

This recipe would be good for mallards, pintails or black ducks.

The state where we live (Massachusetts) has more ice cream parlors than any other in the country. Consequently, it is always easy for us to slip down to the local parlor and buy their freshly made ice cream. If you live where they have more gas stations than any other state you'll find this is still a fine and easy dessert. Unlike some flavors, coffee ice cream seems to be generally good from any source and the hazelnut liqueur makes it *ooh la la*.

DUCKS WITH ROSEMARY AND SAGE

2 roasting ducks
2 tbsp. rosemary
3 tbsp. sage
2 tbsp. salt
2 tbsp. pepper
1 cup duck and chicken livers
  chopped fine
1 small onion
4 strips bacon
3 tbsp. butter
4 cups stock
2 tbsp. cognac

Hopefully the rosemary and sage are fresh; if so chop fine. Add to the salt and pepper. Chop the onion fine and add to the chopped livers. Take half the herb mixture and add it to the onions and livers. Stuff the onion, liver, and herbs into the cavity of each duck and truss. Rub the remaining

122

half of the herb mixture over the skin and add two strips of bacon on to each bird. Roast at 350° for 40 minutes. Remove the bacon and brown for 10 more minutes. Place the ducks onto a heated platter.

Reduce the stock to two cups.

Deglaze a pan with cognac and add the reduced stock. Now remove the livers from the ducks and add it to the stock. Whisk in the butter while heating the liver mixture over low heat. Carve the ducks and pour a little of the sauce over the meat.

FONTINA POLENTA

¾ cup cornmeal
1 small onion (optional)
2 cups milk
6 tbsp. butter
½ cup heavy cream
5 oz. fontina, diced
½ tsp. nutmeg
2- tsp. kosher salt
3 Pepper

If you are using the onion, sauté it in the butter until translucent. Then, in a small saucepan bring the onion, butter and milk to a boil. Add the cornmeal slowly, stirring constantly till thick and the spoon can stand up in it. Be careful as the polenta will spit at you. Remove from the heat and add the cheese, nutmeg and salt. Beat in the cream and pepper. Turn immediately into buttered muffin tins and let rest till set. Remove from the tin and put in a heavy oven-proof pan and cook at 400° for 15 minutes (if you like, you can add a little more cheese to the tops of the polenta muffins before putting them in the oven.)

ZUCCHINI FANS WITH TOMATOES

6 small zucchini
4 small tomatoes
Unsalted butter
Basil
Salt and
pepper

Make four deep cuts into each zucchini. Slice almost to the base and create a fan out of each zucchini. Slice the tomatoes and slip them into the zucchini cuts. Arrange carefully in a buttered baking dish and sprinkle with basil. Dot with butter and bake in a 350° oven for 20 minutes or until tender. Place in a serving dish with a spatula and season with salt and pepper.

**Grilled Sea Ducks
Grilled Vegetables
Garlic Cheese Bread
Poached Pears**

Serves four

GRILLED SEA DUCKS

4   sea ducks, breasted out
1   loaf of day-old French
    bread
2-3 tbsp. bacon or pancetta fat
3   cloves of garlic
½   cup (1 stick) unsalted butter

Slice the French bread and rub each side of the slices with the garlic. Sauté the bread in butter and let cool. Crumble the bread and set aside.

Grill the breasts over a medium hot wood fire for 3-4 minutes per side. Sprinkle the breasts with the bread crumbs and season with salt and pepper.

GRILLED VEGETABLES

2 red peppers
1 eggplant
1 yellow squash
1 zucchini

Roast the red peppers on the grill, turning them till each side gets black. Remove and let cool. Peel off the black skin. Remove the seeds and cut into 1-inch slivers.

Slice the eggplant into ¼-inch thick pieces. Sprinkle both sides of each piece with salt and let stand and drain for 30 minutes. Grill till the grill marks show on each side.

Cut the zucchini and yellow squash into ¼-inch slices and grill until the marks show.

Toss the four vegetables together and sauté in hot butter over a medium heat. Add salt and pepper to taste.

GARLIC CHEESE BREAD

    French bread
1   garlic clove
3   oz. fontina
3   oz. mozzarella

Slice the French bread and rub each piece with the peeled garlic clove. Toast under the broiler. Sliver the fontina and the mozzarella and sprinkle on top of the toast. Run them under the broiler for a minute or two and then season with salt and pepper.

POACHED PEARS

4   ripe pears
2   cups water
1⅓ cups sugar
1   vanilla bean, split
     Several drops of
     lemon juice

Peel the pears with a vegetable peeler and core from the bottom with a melon baller. Rub the peeled pears with lemon juice. In a saucepan combine water, a few drops of lemon juice, and sugar and bring it to a boil. Add the halved vanilla bean and reduce the heat. Simmer for 5 minutes. Then add the pears and continue to simmer for about 10 minutes or until the pears are tender. Remove the pears from the syrup and stand upright on a plate in the refrigerator. The chilled pears can be served with crème anglaise, whipped cream, chocolate shavings, or a liqueur over it.

_____

Grilled Breast of Mallard
Gorganzola Polenta
Cucumber and Radishes
Fresh Fruit

Serves four

This recipe is very much designed for a mallard, particularly a mallard who's been spending his time away from the ocean. I've always been a staunch supporter of the blacks and mallards that live by the sea and honestly believe there is very little difference in taste from those that feast on corn each day. But there is one thing that makes an inland mallard special—the skin. For some reason these ducks have especially good skin. It does seem unfortunate to go to the trouble of plucking a duck just to breast him out, but the skin sautéed separately is delicious.

This recipe might also be recommended for use on a duck hunting camping trip.

GRILLED BREAST OF MALLARD

4   mallards
2-3 tbsp. pancetta or bacon fat

After the ducks have been plucked, skin them and cut the breasts out. Save the skin and pound the breasts to ¼ inch thickness and paint with melted bacon fat.

Cut the skin into strips and sauté in the fat till crispy (about 20 minutes). Chop and set aside.

Grill the breasts over a medium hot wood fire, about 3 minutes a side. Sprinkle the pieces of skin over the breasts and serve.

GORGANZOLA POLENTA

¾   cup cornmeal
1   small onion (optional)
2   cups milk
6   tbsp. butter
½   cup heavy cream
5   oz. gorganzola, diced
½   tsp. nutmeg
2-3 tsp. kosher salt
     Pepper

If you are using the onion, sauté it in the butter until translucent. Then, in a small saucepan bring the onion, butter and milk to a boil. Add the cornmeal slowly, stirring constantly till thick and the spoon can stand up in it. Be careful as the polenta will spit at you. Remove from the heat and add the cheese, nutmeg and salt. Beat in the cream and pepper. Turn immediately into buttered muffin tins and let rest till set. Remove from the tin and put in a heavy oven-proof pan and cook at 400° for 15 minutes (if you like, you can add a little more cheese to the tops of the polenta muffins before putting them in the oven.)

CUCUMBERS AND RADISHES

2 cucumbers
1 bunch radishes
2 tbsp. unsalted butter
  Mint or dill
  Salt and pepper

Clean and slice thickly (⅛-inch thick) the radishes. Peel the cucumbers then cut them in half the long way. Scoop out the seeds and then slice each half into ⅛-inch pieces. Sauté the cucumbers and radishes in the butter. Season with salt and pepper and a little mint or dill.

Stuffed Duck Breasts
Green Beans and Wild Mushrooms
Bibb and Radish Salad
Grapefruit Sabayon

Serves four

My preference in general is to pluck and roast a duck. This is not always desirable, however, if he is quite shot up or the skin has torn for some other reason. This recipe is for just such a dilapidated duck.

Dried wild mushrooms can be purchased in nice little plastic bags now. There certainly is no need to risk life and psyche by trying to collect them if you are unfamiliar with the varieties.

STUFFED DUCK BREASTS

4   ducks, breasted out
1   lb. spinach
¼   cup currants, soaked in a little
      armagnac
¼   cup stock
1   egg
¾   cup bread crumbs
1   tsp. tarragon
1   tbsp. fresh, chopped basil
5   tbsp. unsalted butter
      Salt and pepper

Wash the spinach and put it in a pan with a tight lid over a medium heat for a few minutes until the spinach is just barely limp. Let cool and then chop. Combine the spinach with the currants and their juices, the stock, the egg, the bread crumbs, the tarragon and salt and pepper to taste. Cut a pocket in each duck breast and stuff the spinach mixture into the breast. Oven poach the breasts by sautéing them in the butter for just a few minutes. Place in a buttered baking dish and cut a round of wax paper to fit over the top of the dish and butter it. Press the wax paper over the breasts. Cook for 5 minutes at 400° or until the meat is springy to the touch.

Make a noisette butter by heating the remaining amounts of butter until it turns a hazelnut brown. Pour over the breasts. Season with salt and pepper.

GREEN BEANS WITH WILD MUSHROOMS

1 lb. green beans
1 oz. dried wild mushrooms
2 tbsp. unsalted butter
Salt and pepper

Blanch the green beans and then chill them immediately in ice water. Reconstitute the mushrooms in a little warm water. Rinse the mushrooms in cool water saving the reconstituted juice. Reduce the juice in a sauté pan (be sure not to get any of the mushrooms' grit in the pan) until it is just a glaze on the bottom of the pan. Melt the butter with the glaze and add the mushrooms and beans. Sauté, then season with salt and pepper.

GRAPEFRUIT SABAYON

3 egg yolks
½ cup sugar
½ cup wine or rum
1 tbsp. Grand Marnier
2 pink grapefruits
2 white grapefruits
Pinch of salt

Cut the peel off of the grapefruits making sure to remove all of the white pith. Then slice into rounds and core and seed each round. Arrange attractively in an oven-proof dish.
Make the sabayon by first beating the eggs and sugar together until it lightly ribbons. Add the wine and a pinch of salt. Over a medium-low heat (the pan should never get too hot on the bottom to touch) whisk constantly to incorporate air into the egg, sugar and wine mixture. Once it's thickened blend in the liqueur or lemon juice and pour the sabayon over the grapefruit. Run the dessert under the broiler for a few minutes to just brown the surface.

Duck Salad
Basil Pasta
Cantaloupe Ice

Serves four

Sun-dried tomatoes, listed in the next recipe, are no longer very difficult to find. Most often found in Italian grocery stores or in gourmet shops in
canisters like any other dried fruit, they also are available packed in oil at a
higher cost. They are wonderful and worth whatever price you are asked to
pay. If you cannot find them, this recipe will work without them.

When making a vinaigrette it's nice to know that a mistake of too much
vinegar or lemon can be corrected by adding a little more salt.

Mallard would be a good duck for this recipe.

Homemade pasta is wonderful, although tedious to make (see page 32)
and definitely would be wasted in this recipe. The imported boxed pasta is
suited to heavy sauces and vinaigrettes and can be purchased in delightful
shapes.

Try to use a very ripe cantaloupe for the ice recipe.

DUCK SALAD

4	ducks, roasted
8	slices bacon
2	apples
¾	cup sun-dried tomatoes
2	scallions
⅓	cup olive oil
⅓	cup white wine
2	cloves garlic
½	lb. snow peas
2	cloves garlic
1	tsp. fennel seeds
	Bouquet garni (bay leaf, parsley stems, thyme)
	A few peppercorns
¼	tsp. prepared mustard
½	tbsp. vinegar
	Salt and pepper

130

Roast the four ducks by stuffing each with half an apple and then trussing it . Lay two strips of bacon on each duck and roast in a 350° oven for 50 minutes. Let the ducks cool and then remove the meat from the bones.

Next reconstitute the sun-dried tomatoes. In a small pot combine the peeled garlic cloves, tomatoes, bouquet garni, peppercorns, a few crushed fennel seeds and the olive oil and white wine. Simmer over a low heat until the tomatoes are soft (about 15 minutes). Let cool and dice. Be sure to save the oil and white wine mixture for making the dressing. Add the tomatoes to the pieces of duck meat.

Blanch the snow peas in a large quantity of salted, boiling water for about 30 seconds. Remove from the water and plunge into ice water to maintain the green color. Drain and dry and add to the duck and tomatoes.

Chop the green part of the scallions and add it to the salad with the crushed fennel seeds.

Make a dressing by putting into the blender the juice from the reconstituted tomatoes, the vinegar, and the mustard. Blend on high for 10 seconds. Taste for seasoning and correct. Pour over the duck combination and toss.

BASIL PASTA

1   lb. pasta
1   large bunch fresh basil
⅓   cup vinegar
    Touch of lemon juice
1   cup olive oil
1   tbsp. prepared mustard
2   large cloves garlic
6   oz. goat cheese
    Salt and pepper
    Hot pepper flakes
1   bay leaf

In the cup of olive oil cook the peeled garlic cloves over a medium low heat for about 20 minutes or until the garlic is soft but still holds its shape. Add the bay leaf while it is still hot and let sit overnight.

Make a little vinaigrette with the vinegar, lemon juice, mustard and salt and pepper. Pour the vinaigrette into a blender and add the basil with their stems removed and the olive oil garlic (less the bay leaf). Blend till smooth. Check for seasoning.

Cook the pasta particularly *al dente* (it will absorb the moisture from the basil mixture and become mushy if cooked till soft). Let cool somewhat or it will discolor the beautiful green of the basil. Drain the pasta and toss with the basil vinaigrette. Sprinkle with red pepper flakes and crumbled goat cheese. Decorate with any extra little basil leaves.

CANTALOUPE ICE

2 very ripe cantaloupes
¾ cup confectioners' sugar
    Lemon juice to taste
    A pinch of salt
1 tbsp. white rum
    (Make sure you have
    enough ice and salt for
    your ice cream machine)

Halve the cantaloupes and scoop out the seeds. Now scoop out the fruit and make sure you have about one quart. Puree the cantaloupe in a blender and then add the sugar, salt, and lemon juice sparingly until the mixture tastes right. Now add the rum and make any adjustments for taste. Place the cantaloupe mixture in the canister of your ice cream machine and place in the refreigerator for a couple of hours. Then freeze it in the machine according to the manufacturer's directions. Pack back into the cantaloupe shells if you like.

Grilled Marinated Ducks
Grilled Red Onion
Grilled Mushrooms
Basil Bread
Crème Brulée

Serves four

In all of the bread recipes listed in this book a flour and yeast ball is made first. The purpose of this is to test the yeast and insure that it can make the bread rise. If, however, you are already a bread-maker and set in your ways don't hesitate to use your own basic bread recipe and add the reconstituted basil to the milk or water in the recipe.

This is not a heavy, jelly-like crème brulée. Expect it to be a true custard.

This is a good recipe for widgeon.

GRILLED MARINATED DUCKS

2	ducks, butterflied (see page 211)
2	tbsp. unsalted butter
4	carrots
3	onions
	Parsley stems
	Fresh thyme sprigs
2	lemon slices
1	bay leaf
20	crushed peppercorns
2	tsp. salt
1	bottle red wine

Chop the onion and carrots and sauté in the butter till the onions are translucent. Add the red wine and bring to a simmer. Add the remaining ingredients and pour over the ducks. Let marinate for one or two days turning the breasts every so often.

Dry roast the duck in a preheated oven for 20 minutes at 450°.

Grill over a medium-low fire, starting skin side down on the grill for 15 minutes. Turn over and grill 4 more minutes. Take off grill and rest 5 minutes. Cut in portions to serve.

GRILLED RED ONION

2 red onions
2 tbsp. unsalted butter
Salt and pepper

Slice the onions ¼-inch thick and charcoal grill or broil them lightly for 2–3 minutes per side. Now sauté them quickly in the butter over a medium heat and season with salt and pepper.

Or you can dribble green olive oil over them and serve hot or cold.

GRILLED MUSHROOMS

1 lb. large mushrooms (whole or
   halved)
3 tbsp. unsalted butter
Salt and pepper

Charcoal grill or broil the mushrooms for 3–4 minutes and then sauté them in the butter. Season with salt and pepper.

BASIL BREAD

3 cups all-purpose flour
1 pkg. dry yeast
2 tbsp. basil
1 tsp. salt

In a medium size bowl mix 1 cup of the flour with the yeast and add enough warm water (not hot water) to make a moist and cohesive ball. Fill the bowl with warm water so the ball is covered. Let sit 5 to 15 minutes until the ball pops to the surface. Meanwhile take the remaining amount of flour (this can be all white flour or a mixture such as ⅔ white and ⅓ whole wheat) and put it on top of the counter. Make a trench in the middle of the pile and add the salt. Reconstitute the basil by pouring a little hot water in with it first and stirring then add it to the flour trench. You will need to add more water, a few tablespoons at a time, fluffing it into the flour with your fingers . The mixture should be slightly cohesive but not wet as the yeast/flour ball will be quite wet. When the ball has risen to the surface of the water, scoop it out and set in the middle of your pile of flour. Knead the ball and the flour together and continue to knead for 8 minutes or so. Put the dough in an oiled or floured bowl with a towel over it and place in a warm spot to rise several hours or until double in bulk. Punch down and let rise again or shape and bake in a preheated oven at 425° till done (about 35–40 minutes). Remember it can rise and be punched down four times, after that the yeast dies. Also, after the first rising it can be punched down and left to rise slowly overnight in the refrigerator.

CRÈME BRULÉE

6	eggs
5	tbsp. sugar
3	cups heavy cream (or 1½ cups heavy cream and 1½ cups whipping cream)
1	tbsp. vanilla
½-⅔	cup light brown sugar

Separate the eggs and combine the yolks well with the white sugar and cream. Heat the mixture until very warm over a medium heat stirring constantly. Remove from the flame and add the vanilla. Pour through a strainer into a baking dish. Put the dish into a roasting pan and surround it with an inch or so of boiling water. Bake it in a preheated oven at 300° for 25 minutes or until the custard is just setting around the edges but is still soft in the middle. Remove from the oven and let it sit in the waterbath while it cools. Then refrigerate the custard for at least two hours or overnight. Just before serving sprinkle the custard with the brown sugar and put under a very hot broiler for a few seconds. If you cannot get your broiler hot enough, put the dish in cracked ice so the custard won't cook anymore while the brown sugar forms a nice hard crust. Serve immediately or chill again and serve.

Roasted Duck
Potatoes Steamed with Sage
Bittergreens and Cheese Salad
Tangerine Sorbet

Serves four

A very controversial issue in game cooking is the length of cooking time for ducks. Some people prefer their ducks cooked for 10 or 15 minutes, some for hours. Of course the preference also determines the results. Some like blood red meat, some like leather brown meat. We go with the middle-of-the road system. We prefer to cook our blacks and mallards at 350° for 50 minutes so that they are pink inside but share no risk of being either bloody or leathery. It is, of course, purely a matter of taste not only specifically with ducks but with any meat. If you are uncertain how you prefer your ducks and don't have a large quantity to experiment with, try it my way. This recipe is good for blacks, mallards and pintails.

Be sure to use the liqueur suggested in the sorbet; it makes a difference.

ROASTED DUCK

4 ducks
2 carrots
2 onions
1 celery stick
6 parsley stems
2 tbsp. bacon fat
2 cups white wine
1 bay leaf
4 cloves garlic, peeled and crushed
8 strips of bacon
8 sprigs of thyme
4 tbsp. unsalted butter
Salt and pepper

Chop the carrots, celery, onion, and parsley stems fine and sauté in fat in the roasting pan. Set ducks on this bed of vegetables. Place a sprig of thyme and two strips of bacon on each duck. Add the white wine and bring to a simmer. Now add the garlic, bay leaf, and salt and pepper. Roast in a preheated oven at 350° for 40 minutes, discard the bacon and continue cooking for 10 minutes more to brown them. Remove the ducks and place on a heated platter. Purée the vegetables and juices in the blender, first removing the bay leaf. Strain the purée and return it to the stove whisking in the butter. Season with salt and pepper.

Carve the ducks pouring a little of the sauce over each serving.

POTATOES STEAMED WITH SAGE

12 little red potatoes (or what
   seems the right number for four
   folks)
1 tbsp. crumbled dried sage
4 tbsp. unsalted butter
¼ cup freshly grated parmesan
   cheese
   Salt and pepper

Wash and cut the potatoes in half (if they are big). Place the potatoes on a vegetable steaming rack and sprinkle with sage. Put the rack into a saucepan with just a ½ inch of boiling water. Steam covered for 5 minutes or until tender. Put the potatoes into a serving dish and pat with butter. Sprinkle with parmesan cheese and salt and pepper to taste. Toss and serve.

BITTERGREENS AND CHEESE SALAD

   Escarole, chicory and arugula
   Bibb lettuce
   French bread
5 tbsp. unsalted butter
4 strips of bacon
3 oz. blue cheese
   Vinaigrette
   Garlic clove
   Salt and pepper

Wash and dry the lettuce and break into bite size pieces. Slice the bread into 1-inch square pieces, rub with garlic, dry in a 300° oven, and then fry in butter. Set aside. Cut the bacon into 1-inch pieces and fry till medium done, not quite crisp. Cut the cheese into small cubes. Combine the lettuce, bacon and cheese and toss with the vinaigrette. Add the croutons and check for seasoning. Serve.

TANGERINE SORBET

10–12 tangerines
1 cup sugar
 Pinch of salt
1 tbsp. Mandarin Napoleon
 liqueur (tangarine liqueur)
 Splash of lemon juice
 (Remember to have enough
 ice and salt for your ice
 cream freezer, too).

Squeeze enough tangerines so you have 1 quart of juice. Bring sugar and half a cup of water to a boil and simmer for 5 minutes. Let cool. Add the sugar syrup to the fruit juice as needed to please your taste. Add the salt and lemon juice to help the taste and then pour in the liqueur. Chill the mixture in the canister from your ice cream maker. Then freeze according to the ice cream machine's directions.

Minted Roast Duck with Potatoes, Carrots and Turnips
Green Salad
Olive Oil and Sauternes Cake

Serves four

Wild creatures tend to have very little fat. And what fat they do have is not marbled throughout the meat but stored in certain specific locations. It also is fat which, if cooked with the bird, will harm the taste (see page 190). Theoretically the fat has all been cleaned out of the bird and in order to cook it so it isn't dried out you must add good-tasting fat or a liquid to the bird while cooking. This recipe suggests a nice technique for doing that and is particularly good for black ducks.

The olive oil and Sauternes cake doesn't sound very tasty. It is wonderful. It is from Alice Waters' Chez Panisse Menu Cookbook.

You know how to make the salad.

MINTED ROAST DUCK WITH POTATOES, CARROTS AND TURNIPS

2   ducks for roasting
½   cup (1 stick) unsalted butter
1½ tbsp. dried mint, reconstituted
      in a little hot water
4   potatoes
4   large turnips
4   carrots
2   tbsp. bacon fat
      Salt, pepper, and a pinch of
      cayenne

Whip the butter. Add the mint, salt, pepper and cayenne to taste and whip again. Carefully pull the skin of the duck slightly away from the meat and slip the butter between the breasts and the skin, covering as much surface as possible.

Peel and quarter the potatoes. Peel the carrots and cut into 2-inch chunks. Peel and halve the turnips. Sauté all three vegetables in the bacon fat. Place the sautéed vegetables in a roasting pan with the ducks and cook at 450° for 10 minutes. Turn the oven down to 325° and finish cooking, about 35 minutes more.

OLIVE OIL AND SAUTERNES CAKE

5 eggs plus 2 egg whites
¾ cup sugar
1 tbsp. mixed grated orange and
   lemon peel
1 cup sifted flour
½ teaspoon salt
½ cup good quality Sauternes
½ cup plus 2 tbsp. extra virgin
   olive oil

Preheat the oven to 375°. Separate the 5 eggs and beat the egg yolks with ¾ cup sugar in a bowl with a whisk for 3 to 5 minutes until light colored and well-beaten. Add the orange and lemon peel and set aside.

Combine 1 cup sifted flour and ½ teaspoon salt, then add bit by bit to the sugar-egg mixture, beating continually until it is all incorporated. Add the Sauternes and olive oil in the same fashion.

Beat the 5 egg whites and 2 additional egg whites until they stand in stiff peaks, then fold them into the mixture thoroughly.

Pour this batter into an 8-inch spring-form pan whose bottom has been lined with parchment and whose entire interior has been well buttered. Bake for 20 minutes, rotating the cake if necessary to insure even cooking. After 20 minutes lower the temperature to 325° and bake for another 20 minutes. Then turn off the oven, cover the cake with a round of parchment, and leave the cake in the closed oven for 10 minutes more while the cake deflates like a fallen souffle.

Remove the cake from the oven, invert it onto a flat surface, remove from the spring-form pan, allow it to cool completely.

This cake can be stored, well sealed, in the refrigerator. Serve with fresh peaches and a glass of Sauternes.

Duck Roasted with Red Pepper Butter
Persillade Potatoes
Sautéed Green Beans and Cherry Tomatoes
Almond Cake

Serves four

Sweet roasted red peppers come in nasty little jars from the super-market. And they do not taste very good. When you roast them yourself they take on a nice charcoal taste and aren't watery from sitting in a jar. Not only are they delicious in the butter as suggested here, but are great in salads. They also can be kept in the refrigerator with a little olive oil for instant salad and sandwich use.

The Sautéed Green Beans and Cherry Tomatoes is something you know how to do. Blanch the beans and prick the tomatoes with a pin before sautéing for best results.

DUCK ROASTED WITH RED PEPPER BUTTER

4 duck breasts, butterflied (see page 211)
1 cup (2 sticks) unsalted butter, softened
½ cup roasted and peeled red pepper
1 garlic clove, chopped fine
½ tsp. fresh ground pepper
Salt

Preheat the broiler. On a cookie sheet place 2 or 3 red peppers as close as possible to the heat turning them till charred on all sides. Let cool. While the peppers cool remove all charred black skin. Whip the butter till soft and light. Chop the peppers fine and add them, the garlic, pepper and salt to the butter. Whip together and then let sit in the freezer for several hours. Remove the butter from the freezer an hour or so before serving. Grill the butterflied breasts and put several slices of compound butter on the meat. Serve.

PERSILLADE POTATOES

2 large potatoes
2 garlic cloves
½ bunch parsley
2 tbsp. bacon fat or butter
Salt and pepper

Chop the parsley and garlic fine and mix together. Peel and slice the potatoes and then sauté them in bacon fat over a medium heat for a few minutes, then with the lid on for five or so minutes. Remove the lid and add the parsley and garlic mixture and cook for several more minutes. Season with salt and pepper and serve.

ALMOND CAKE

¾ cup almonds
6 tbsp. unsalted butter
⅔ cup sugar
3 eggs
½ cup sifted all-purpose flour
3 tbsp. brandy
Dusting of confectioners' sugar

Roast the almonds on a cookie sheet in a 300° oven for about 20 minutes or until they are a nice golden tan. Be sure to shake the almonds often while cooking so they do not get over-done. Chop the almonds very fine. Or this can be done in your food processor.

Melt the butter and when cooled stir in the eggs and sugar. Then add the flour, almonds, and brandy.

Butter and flour an 8-inch square pan and pour the batter into it. Bake at 325° for 20 minutes or until a skewer pulls out clean when you stick it in the center of the cake. Let cool in the pan, then cut into squares and dust with the confectioners' sugar.

Sea Duck Fricassee
Fennel, Mint, Cucumber, Radish Salad
Fried Polenta
Fresh Fruit

Serves four

One problem with duck hunting if you live by an ocean is that the most plentiful ducks are sometimes not the best tasting. The sea ducks that feed on fish and shellfish are a continual challenge to the gourmet cook. How do you prepare them so the fish taste is masked but the good game duck taste comes through? In addition to recipes such as these which are heavy on the masking there are a few home techniques of exorcising the fish taste from the duck meat. One such technique which I can vouch for is to breast out the bird and cook the pieces in near-boiling milk for a few minutes and then sauté in butter and serve as an *hors d'oeuvre*. But for a full main course you might try the following.

SEA DUCK FRICASSEE

4 ducks, breasted out
2 onions, chopped fine
4 carrots, sliced
1 leek, chopped fine
2 large tomatoes, skinned, seeded
   and chopped
2 cups stock
2 tsp. thyme
4 tbsp. unsalted butter
Salt and pepper

Sauté the onions, leeks, and carrots till the onions are translucent. Add the stock and bring to a boil. Let bubble on medium-low heat until the liquid has been reduced by half. Add the duck breasts and thyme and reduce the heat, cover with a piece of foil pressed down to touch the surface of the meat. Simmer over a low heat for 10 minutes or when the breasts feel springy to the touch. Remove the breasts and purée the vegetables with the liquid in a blender or food processor. Return the purée to the heat and reduce it to thicken if necessary. Whisk in the butter and add the tomatoes and duck breasts and heat for a few seconds. Season to taste and serve immediately.

143

FENNEL, MINT, CUCUMBER, RADISH SALAD

1 head fennel
1 bunch radishes
2 cucumbers
Several sprigs of mint
1 garlic clove
¼ cup olive oil
Salt and pepper

Trim, core and cut the fennel. Wash and slice the cucumbers and radishes. Chop the mint and garlic finely and add to the vegetables. Pour the olive oil over it all and season with salt and pepper. Toss and serve.

FRIED POLENTA

1 cup cornmeal
½ cup (1 stick) butter
1 cup water
3 cups milk
½ tsp. nutmeg
Fat to fry in (bacon, pancetta or butter)
1 onion
Salt and pepper

Chop the onion very fine and sauté it in the butter till translucent. Add the milk and bring it to a boil. Combine the cornmeal and water and stir with a fork to mix it, then add it to the boiling milk and onion mixture. Stir continuously until the mixture is so thick the spoon stands up in it. Remove it from the heat and add the nutmeg and season with salt and pepper. Grease a cookie sheet and spread the polenta ½ to ¼-inch thick on it. Let stand until cool and slightly hardened. Now cut with cookie cutters and fry the shapes in the fat till they are lightly brown. Serve.

Sea Duck with Pancetta and Prosciutto
Roast Potatoes with Rosemary
Fresh Green Peas
Kiwi Ice

Serves four

Fresh green peas are, of course, a springtime item so this menu is intended for that lone duck saved in the freezer from last fall's hunt. Otherwise Birdseye's Tender Tiny Green Peas are okay.

SEA DUCK WITH PANCETTA AND PROSCIUTTO

4 skinned duck breasts, sliced into
   two flat pieces as if for scallopini
4 oz. pancetta
4 slices prosciutto
2 tbsp. parsley, chopped fine
   Salt and pepper

Dice the pancetta into ⅛-inch pieces and then sauté till almost crisp. Remove from pan with a slotted spoon and set aside. Sauté the duck breasts in the hot fat and remove when just barely done (remember they'll keep cooking after they've been removed from the pan). Let the breasts cool slightly and slice the pieces on the diagonal. While the duck is cooking julienne the proscuitto and sauté it quickly for a few minutes. Add the cooked pancetta, duck meat and parsley and toss. Season with salt and pepper and serve.

ROAST POTATOES WITH ROSEMARY

16 little red potatoes
4 tbsp. melted, unsalted butter or
   olive oil
   Rosemary
   Salt and pepper

Paint the potatoes with the melted butter and sprinkle liberally with rosemary. Roast in the oven for about 35 minutes at 350° or until they are tender. Season with salt and pepper.

145

KIWI ICE

24 kiwi (approximately)
1 cup sugar
  Pinch of salt
1 tbsp. vodka
  (Remember to have
  enough ice and salt
  for your ice cream
  freezer, too).

Scoop out the insides of the kiwi and purée in the blender. You should have about 1 quart of purée. Boil half a cup of water and add the sugar and cook for 5 minutes. Let cool. Add the sugar syrup to the fruit juice as needed to please your taste. Add salt and lemon juice to help the taste if need be and then pour in the vodka. Chill the mixture in the canister from your ice cream maker. Then freeze according to the ice cream machine's directions.

Sea Duck With Anchovy Butter
Olive Oil and Salt Bread
Soup in a Pumpkin
Figs in Rum

Serves four

There is another home remedy for fishy tasting ducks which I have heard used several times but have never tried myself. By soaking the duck meat in 1 teaspoon salt and 1 teaspoon baking soda to 2 cups water for about an hour the fishiness is gone. It may be a method to attempt before trying this recipe.

SEA DUCK WITH ANCHOVY BUTTER

4   skinned duck breasts
2   anchovies, rinsed in cold water
⅓   cup nicoise olives, pitted and
     chopped fine
1   onion, sliced
½   cup (1 stick) unsalted butter
1   tbsp. olive oil
⅓   cup parsley stems
¼   cup plus 1 tbsp. brandy
¼   cup red wine
     Salt and pepper

Sauté the onion in the oil until translucent. Remove from heat and add parsley stems and ¼ cup each of wine and brandy. Whisk and place in a container with the breasts to marinate overnight.

Make a compound butter by whipping the butter till soft, add the anchovies, olives, a tablespoon of brandy and a little fresh ground pepper. Chill for at least 1 hour and taste for seasoning.

Grill the breasts and serve with a dollop of butter.

OLIVE OIL AND SALT BREAD

3 cups all-purpose flour
1 pkg. dry yeast
2 tbsp. thyme
1 tsp. salt
1 tbsp. kosher salt
¼ cup good green olive oil

In a medium size bowl mix 1 cup of the flour with the yeast and add enough warm water (not hot water) to make a moist and cohesive ball. Fill the bowl with warm water so the ball is covered. Let sit 5 to 15 minutes until the ball pops to the surface. Meanwhile take the remaining amount of flour (this can be all white flour or a mixture such as ⅔ white and ⅓ whole wheat) and put it on top of the counter. Make a trench in the middle of the pile and add the salt. Reconstitute the thyme by pouring a little water in with it first and then add it to the flour trench. You will need to add more water, fluffing it into the flour with your fingers. The mixture should be slightly cohesive but not wet as the yeast/flour ball will be quite wet. When the ball has risen to the surface of the water, scoop it out and set in the middle of your pile of flour. Knead the ball and the flour together and continue to knead for 8 minutes or so. Put the dough in an oiled or floured bowl with a towel over it and place in a warm spot and let rise two hours or until doubled in bulk. Punch down and shape into a round, flat pancake about 8–12 inches wide. Let rise again and carefully poke ¼-inch holes all around the top of the bread with the end of a wooden spoon. Fill the holes with the olive oil (or you can use walnut oil) and sprinkle with the kosher salt. Bake in a preheated oven at 425° till done (about 35–40 minutes). Remember it can rise and be punched down four times, after that the yeast dies. Also, after the first rising it can be punched down and left to rise slowly overnight in the refrigerator.

SOUP IN A PUMPKIN

1 perfect little pumpkin
   which will fit in your oven
   and weighs about 6 lbs.
1 onion, chopped
   Bay leaf
   Several parsley stems
   Pinch of thyme
½ cup cream
   Croutons
   Chopped parsley
   Salt and pepper
½ cup (1 stick) unsalted butter
5 cups chicken stock

Scoop out the pumpkin. Discard the seeds and string and save the flesh. Be sure not to scoop too close to the skin. Cut the pumpkin flesh into small chunks and sauté it in the butter along with the onion until the pumpkin is soft. Add the stock, herbs, and parsley stems. Season with salt and pepper and let cook until the mixture is quite soft. **Remove bay leaf.** Purée in the blender or a food processor and then strain. Add the cream and check for seasoning. Return the pumpkin soup to the pumpkin shell and cook in the oven for 40 minutes at 350°. Garnish with the croutons and chopped parsley and serve scraping the pumpkin shell sides as you ladle the soup into the bowls.

FIGS IN RUM

2 lbs. fresh figs
1 cup sugar
1 cup water
4 tbsp. rum
1 vanilla bean
   Pinch of thyme or a sprig of
   fresh thyme
1 cup heavy cream

Wash and drain the figs. Simmer the water and sugar together for 5 minutes then add the figs and vanilla bean. Cook slowly over a low heat for 1 hour. Remove from the heat and let cool. Add the rum and cover the fruit tightly. Let it all sit in the refrigerator for two days. Whip the cream and serve on top of the figs.

Marinated Duck Breasts
Plain Roast Potatoes
Julienned Celery and Zucchini
Strawberry Tart

Serves four

When I first started to hunt and to cook wild game it seemed almost sacrilegious to skin ducks and marinate them. I have since learned that those of us who are fortunate to do a lot of hunting and hunt hard throughout the season don't always end up with the finest specimen of bird. There, upon occasion, are edible ducks that need some help either because they are badly shot up or have endured a harsh winter. This recipe is for just such a duck.

There are also some ducks which are are simply inedible no matter what you do to them. There was a friend of ours who had come to visit from Alaska. John has since become quite a good friend, but at the time we were new to each other and new to our mutual hunting ethics. I knew him to be quite a proficient hunter and outdoorsman. And I assumed that anyone from Alaska must be a subsistence hunter inclined to saving and using everything, from beaks to feet. We sat in our Boston apartment after a long day's hunt, cleaning ducks. John pulled at the feathers of the last duck and after several pulls revealed green skin on the poor little black duck. I was horrified when I saw it, not so much from the sight of it but at the the thought that this backwoodsman would probably want to cook and eat him anyway. Pleased I definitely was when I saw John's plucking slow to a stop and the little carcass drop into the garbage can. "We throw those out in Alaska," was all he said. We throw them out in Boston, too. And when in doubt I'd throw any duck out rather than risk the memory of a bad taste or worse.

MARINATED DUCK BREASTS

4 skinned duck breasts
8 toasted and crushed juniper
  berries
1 tbsp. rosemary
10 peppercorns, crushed
4 oz. cognac
4 oz. pine nuts
3 tbsp. unsalted butter

Combine the juniper berries, peppercorns, rosemary and cognac in a bowl and place the skinned breasts in it to marinate 24 hours. Be sure to turn them in the marinade every so often.

Sauté the pine nuts in a tablespoon of the butter until light brown and remove from the pan. Now add the remaining two tablespoons of butter and sauté the duck until done. Serve with the pine nuts sprinkled on top.

JULIENNED CELERY AND ZUCCHINI

6 stalks celery
1 zucchini
2 tbsp. unsalted butter
  Salt and pepper

Scrape the outside skin of the celery stalks with a vegetable peeler (not the tender inside stalks) and cut into 2-inch lengths. Now julienne into ⅛-inch matchsticks. Cut the zucchini into 2-inch chunks and julienne into ⅛-inch sticks. Sauté the celery and zucchini together in butter till they are hot but still crisp. Season with salt and pepper.

STRAWBERRY TART

1   sheet Pepperidge Farm Puff
    Pastry or your own
1   tbsp. butter
2   tbsp. sugar
2   pints strawberries
½   pint heavy cream
2   tbsp. currant jam
½   tbsp. Grand Marnier
3   tbsp. sour cream

Preheat the oven at 425° for at least 20 minutes.

Roll out the pastry and fit into a heavily buttered porcelain tart or quiche dish. Roll the rolling pin over the top to cut the extra pastry off the edges. Let rest in the refrigerator for 1 hour. Prick the pastry with a fork and then flatten a piece of foil over it. Put beans, peas, or pastry weights on top of the foil. Cook in the lower part of the hot oven for 7 minutes then carefully open the oven and remove the foil and weights. Sprinkle with sugar and continue cooking for at least 5 minutes until the crust is a light brown with a shiny, caramelized surface. Then remove from the oven. Slide the pastry out of the dish onto a cake rack to cool completely. Whip the cream. About half way through whipping add the Grand Marnier (Framboise is good, too) and the sour cream. Spread over the bottom of the pastry shell. Arrange the strawberries on top of the cream attractively (raspberries, blueberries or any fruit are good also). Melt the currant jam over a low flame. Remove and let cool slightly. Add a dash of the liqueur you used in the cream. With a 2-inch pastry brush, paint the strawberries with the jam mixture. Serve immediately as it will become soggy if you try to hold it.

Grilled Lemon Duck
Grated Zucchini
Sautéed Cherry Tomatoes
Charcoal Grilled Bread
Pear Cake

Serves four

The ducks in this recipe must be butterflied. This is not some unusual bird/animal act but rather a method of preparing the duck so it will cook completely evenly. By flattening the bird out to bake he is less likely to dry out in the legs and breast. Butterflying can be done to any duck (and upland birds, too) but is particularly good for the smaller ducks. Teal or wood ducks are suggested for this recipe.

GRILLED LEMON DUCK

  6 lemons, sliced very thin
  4 ducks
  1 sweet red onion
      Olive oil
      Oregano
      Salt and pepper

Peel and slice the onion and lay it on the bottom of a large roasting pan. Butterfly (see page 211) and flatten the breasts of the ducks and season with salt, pepper and oregano. Set the breasts skin side up on top of the onions and completely cover with the lemon slices. Paint with olive oil, cover and refrigerate overnight.

One hour before cooking remove the ducks from the refrigerator. Take the lemon slices off and reserve (also reserve the onion slices). Baste the duck again with the oil. Grill the breasts, bone side first, quickly on both sides and return to the onions. Replace the lemon slices and baste again with olive oil. Roast at 350° for 35 minutes. (Make any necessary adjustments for time and temperature depending on size of the bird). Season with salt and pepper.

GRATED ZUCCHINI

6 medium zucchini
2 tbsp. unsalted butter
  Salt and pepper
1 lb. spinach
1 shallot, chopped

Grate the zucchini coarsely. Put it in a strainer and sprinkle with salt. Let stand and drain for 20 minutes. Meanwhile, wash spinach and shake dry, barely wilt over a medium-low flame with the lid on for a second. Drain the spinach and let it cool then chop. Squeeze the water out of the zucchini. Sauté the shallot in butter over a medium-low heat then add the zucchini. Add the spinach. Stirring continuously heat the vegetables over medium heat until hot to the touch. Add salt and pepper to taste and serve.

SAUTÉED CHERRY TOMATOES

24 cherry tomatoes
2 tbsp. unsalted butter
  Several sprigs of fresh basil
  (or any other fresh herb
  you may have. Dried
  herbs will work, too)
  Salt and pepper

Prick each cherry tomato with a pin to prevent the tomato skins from bursting and remove the green tops. Sauté in the butter until hot and sprinkle with the chopped herb and salt and pepper. Serve.

CHARCOAL GRILL BREAD

1 loaf of French bread
1 garlic clove
  About ½ cup good green olive oil

Slice the bread into ½-inch pieces and rub each side with the garlic. Grill over a medium-low fire and then pour a little of the olive oil on each piece.

PEAR CAKE

2   eggs
¼   cup milk
2   tsp. vanilla, pear liqueur or
    rum
1   cup sugar
    Pinch of salt
1½ cups flour
1   orange, grate the rind
2   lbs. fresh pears
    Butter to grease the cake pan
½   cup unflavored bread crumbs

Preheat the oven to 350°. Beat the eggs, milk and vanilla (or liqueur) together in a bowl. Add the sugar, salt and orange rind and continue beating. Now blend in the flour. Peel the pears and cut them in half. Scoop out the seeds and core and slice into pieces no more than 1 inch thick. Add to the egg, flour, and sugar mixture. Grease a 9-inch cake pan with butter and then sprinkle the bread crumbs into it. Shake the crumbs all about and then empty the pan of any excess crumbs. Pour the batter into the cake tin and level it with a spoon. Bake in the preheated oven for 45 minutes or until it is a light brown. Let it cool and then remove it from the pan. The pear cake can be eaten lukewarm or cold. Good with a lightly whipped cream, too.

Smoked Goose Salad
Butternut Squash Soup
Sun-dried Tomato Bread
Chocolate Cake

Serves four

The next two menus involve using smoked goose. I like to smoke our geese because I never really found a method of roasting which made them taste as romantic as the recipe made them sound. Geese are big, tough birds in general and even though they are terrific fun to shoot, I'd rather eat a black duck any day. So the smoking helps considerably. There are, of course, several types of smoking methods and many types of smokers. We use a hot smoke technique and a charcoal cooker. The charcoal cookers are a little bit more difficult to control than electric ones but definitely produce the desired results. We suggest following the manufacturer's directions on how to rig the cooker. Use a piece of green, fruit-tree wood on the coals; this will affect the taste. Use beer or wine in the water. It appears to have absolutely no effect on the taste but esthetically is much more pleasing. Do not smoke the goose for as long as is recommended. We usually do our geese for only an hour even though much more is recommended. The length of time is greatly affected by the outside temperature where the smoker sits. Just remember that it is always possible to cook something more, but impossible to uncook an over-done bird.

SMOKED GOOSE SALAD

1 smoked goose
  Rind from 1 orange
4 celery stalks
1 apple
½ cup walnuts, toasted and
  chopped fine
  Lettuce leaves (Boston or Bibb
  or any type that would make a
  nice bed of lettuce)
½ cup walnut oil
1 tsp. shallots, chopped fine
1 tbsp. vinegar
1 tsp. prepared mustard
1 tsp. tarragon
  Salt and pepper

Remove the meat from the bones of the goose. The skin of a smoked goose is worth saving as it contains much of the flavor so leave it on the meat. Cut the meat into bite-size pieces and set aside. Peel the orange making sure not to get any of the white pith. Blanch and julienne the peel. Set aside. Peel the celery stalks and apple and cut into nice size pieces. Toast the walnuts. Combine the goose, orange rind, apple, celery and walnuts. Make a vinaigrette in the blender with the remaining ingredients and pour over the goose mixture and toss. Check for seasoning and serve on a bed of lettuce.

BUTTERNUT SQUASH SOUP

1 butternut squash
¾ cup unsalted butter
1 tsp. nutmeg
1 tbsp. thyme
2 cups chicken stock
1 cup heavy cream
  Salt and pepper

Peel the squash so there is no beige, hard skin on it. Remove the seeds and any of the stringy darker insides with a spoon. Cube and sauté the squash in ½ cup of butter over a medium-low heat until the squash is very soft. Purée the squash in a blender or food processor and strain it back into the sauté pan. Add the remaining ¼ cup butter, thyme, and stock and cook gently, stirring with a wire whisk, until all ingredients are well combined and hot. Add the cream and stir for another minute or two. Check for salt and pepper and serve.

SUN-DRIED TOMATO BREAD

3 cups all-purpose flour
1 pkg. dry yeast
½ cup sun-dried tomatoes
  Sprig of thyme
⅓ cup pitted black olives
1 tsp. salt
¼ cup wine
¼ cup olive oil
2 garlic cloves

In a medium size bowl mix 1 cup of the flour with the yeast and add enough warm water (not hot water) to make a moist and cohesive ball. Fill the bowl with warm water so the ball is covered. Let sit 5 to 15 minutes until the ball pops to the surface. Meanwhile take the remaining amount of flour (this can be all white flour or a mixture such as ⅔ white and ⅓ whole wheat) and put it on top of the counter. Make a trench in the middle of the pile and add the salt. Reconstitute the tomatoes by cooking them in the oil, thyme, and wine over a medium-low heat until they are soft. Let them cool and then chop them coarsely. Add both the olive and the reconstituted tomatoes to the flour trench. You will also need to add a couple tablespoons of water fluffing it into the flour with your fingers. The mixture should be slightly cohesive but not wet as the yeast/flour ball will be quite wet. When the ball has risen to the surface of the water, scoop it out and set in the middle of your pile of flour. Knead the ball and the flour together and continue to knead for 8 minutes or so. Put the dough in an oiled or floured bowl with a towel over it and place in a warm spot to rise 2 hours or until doubled in bulk. Punch down and let rise again or shape and bake in a preheated oven at 425° till done (about 35-40 minutes). Remember it can rise and be punched down four times, after that the yeast dies. Also, after the first rising it can be punched down and left to rise slowly overnight in the refrigerator.

CHOCOLATE CAKE

½ lb. (2 sticks) unsalted butter
½ lb. unsweetened chocolate
(the better the chocolate, the
better the cake)
1½ cup sugar
10 eggs, separated
1 tbsp. lemon juice
2 tbsp. orange liqueur
(Cointreau)
1 tbsp. vanilla
Pinch of salt
Sprinkle of confectioners' sugar

Combine the butter and chocolate in a saucepan and melt them over a low flame. Add the vanilla, lemon juice and liqueur. Remove from the heat. Beat together the egg yolks and sugar until they ribbon lightly and then combine with the chocolate mixture. Beat the egg whites until they support a whole raw egg without sinking and then mix in ⅓ of the whites into the chocolate mixture. Fold in the remaining whites.

Butter and flour a 10-inch spring form pan. Cut a 10-inch round of wax paper and butter and flour that, placing it on the bottom of the spring form pan. Pour the cake batter into the pan and bake in a preheated oven of 250° for 2½ hours. Let cool completely and remove it from the pan. Sprinkle with confectioners' sugar.

Smoked Goose In Cold Pasta Salad
Pepperoni Bread
Almond Cake

Serves four

The goose and pasta salad in this menu requires the use of grapes. Grapes, generally speaking, should be peeled if they are to be used in a cold salad. However, you will notice I have not said that here. I envision this menu for a Sunday supper with one's spouse and favorite friends and where a modest amount of effort over the meal is desirable. Peeling grapes for a meal like this seems silly. If, however, the Queen of England is coming for lunch it is advisable to peel the grapes as they will blend better in the salad.

SMOKED GOOSE IN COLD PASTA SALAD

1   smoked goose
½ cup green, seedless grapes
½ cup red grapes
½ lb. pasta
½ cup hazelnut oil
2   tbsp. red wine
3   tbsp. cream
1   tsp. prepared mustard
    Salt and pepper

Remove the meat from the bones of the goose. The skin of a smoked goose is good and can be left with the meat. Cut the meat into bite-size pieces and set aside. Combine all the remaining ingredients but the pasta in the blender to make a vinaigrette. Cook the pasta *al dente* and let cool but not become cold. Toss the pasta, goose, grapes and vinaigrette together and check for seasoning.

PEPPERONI BREAD

3   cups all-purpose flour
1   pkg. dry yeast
⅔ cup pepperoni, chopped
1   tsp. salt

In a medium size bowl mix 1 cup of the flour with the yeast and add enough warm water (not hot water) to make a moist and cohesive ball. Fill the bowl with warm water so the ball is covered. Let sit 5 to 15 minutes until the ball pops to the surface. Meanwhile take the remaining amount of flour (this can be all white flour or a mixture such as ⅔ white and ⅓ whole wheat) and put it on top of the counter. Make a trench in the middle of the pile and add the salt. Add the chopped pepperoni to the flour trench. You will need to add more water fluffing it into the flour with your fingers The mixture should be slightly cohesive but not wet as the yeast/flour ball will be quite wet. When the ball has risen to the surface of the water, scoop it out and set in the middle of your pile of flour. Knead the ball and the flour together and continue to knead for 8 minutes or so. Put the dough in an oiled or floured bowl with a towel over it and place in a warm spot to rise 2 hours or until doubled in bulk. Punch down and let rise again or shape and bake in a preheated oven at 425° till done (about 35-40 minutes). Remember it can rise and be punched down four times, after that the yeast dies. Also, after the first rising it can be punched down and left to rise slowly overnight in the refrigerator.

ALMOND CAKE

¾ cup almonds
6 tbsp. unsalted butter
⅔ cup sugar
3 eggs
½ cup sifted all-purpose flour
3 tbsp. brandy
Dusting of confectioners' sugar

Roast the almonds on a cookie sheet in a 325° oven for about 20 minutes or until they are a nice golden tan. Be sure to shake the almonds often while cooking so they do not get over-done. Chop the almonds very fine.

This can be done in your food processor if you prefer.

Melt the butter and when cooled stir in the eggs and sugar. Then add the flour, almonds, and brandy.

Butter and flour an 8-inch square pan and pour the batter into it. Bake at 350° for 20 minutes or until a skewer pulls out clean when you stick it in the center of the cake. Let cool in the pan, then cut into squares and dust with the confectioners' sugar.

Christmas Goose Anytime
Pignolis and Raisin Cognac Stuffing
Sautéed Mustard Greens
Cooked Apples
Cornsticks
Good Floating Island

Serves four

Despite the fact my taste buds prefer smoked goose, my mind and heart belong to Dickens. Nothing sounds better than a roast goose. Maybe it's because I expect so much that I've been disappointed but also because so many recipes for goose have clearly never been designed for a wild goose. Wild geese are fatless and dry out easily when cooked if they are not basted and stuffed with other types of fat. They do not need to be cooked for hours; quite the contrary. Also, the cavity of the bird must be meticulously cleaned if you plan to use a stuffing (which is desirable to aid in keeping the meat moist) as blood will not enhance the taste of any stuffing I know about. (I have suggested making more than enough stuffing in this recipe so some can be cooked outside of the bird since not always can we be sure the goose is free of blood.) Also, I'd suggest not shooting at the lead bird in the vee as he is the toughest and oldest of all the birds and will not taste as good. (As I write this I smile. I'd like to meet the enthusiastic hunter that can resist and be patient enough to not take aim at the lead goose.) Hope for a shot at a lone goose and then try this very nice recipe.

CHRISTMAS GOOSE ANYTIME

1   Canada goose (about 6 or 7 lbs. dressed)
Stuffing ingredients:
5   tbsp. pignolis nuts, toasted
¼   cup golden raisins, soaked in hot cognac
1   lb. sweet Italian sausage, chopped
1½ tsp. fennel seeds
¼   tsp. dried thyme
     Salt and pepper
1   small celery stick, chopped fine
1   cup onion, chopped fine
¼   cup cognac
1   egg
½   cup (1 stick) unsalted butter
1½ cup raw rice, cooked
¼   cup chopped parsley
1   additional stick of butter plus cheese cloth to cover the bird

To make the stuffing sauté the onion, celery, sausage and fennel seeds together in the butter till everything looks a light brown. Add the cognac, raisins, nuts, rice, parsley, thyme and toss with salt and pepper. Let cool. Beat the egg and mix into the stuffing. Pack ½ of the stuffing or so into the cavity of the bird and truss him tightly. Melt the remaining stick of butter and soak the cheese cloth in it and spread over the goose. Roast at 350° for about an hour or 10 minutes per pound, basting frequently.

Place the other half of the stuffing mixture in a baking dish and cook in the same oven with the goose for the last ½ hour of the bird's roasting.

SAUTÉED MUSTARD GREENS

1 bunch mustard greens
2 strips of bacon
Salt and pepper

Remove any of the large stems (larger than a pencil) from the mustard greens and wash the greens. Fry the bacon until almost crisp and remove from the pan. Add the mustard greens to the frying pan with the bacon fat still in it and cook quickly with the lid on for a few minutes till wilted. Chop up the bacon and add it to the greens. Season with salt and pepper.

COOKED APPLES

4 apples
3 tbsp. unsalted butter
1 tbsp. calvados
¼ cup cream
Salt and pepper

Make noisette butter by melting the butter over a medium-high heat in a frying pan until the butter has turned a light brown (remember it continues to darken after it is taken from the heat). Meanwhile peel and dice the apples. Cook them in the butter until just tender on a medium heat. Turn the heat to high, add the calvados and let the heat evaporate it. Pour in the cream and cook a few minutes until the cream has thickened. Season with salt and pepper.

CORNSTICKS

1½ cups cornmeal
2 tsp. baking powder
1 tsp. salt
¼ cup flour
2 tbsp. sugar
2 eggs
1 cup buttermilk
3 tbsp. bacon drippings

Sift together the cornmeal, baking powder, salt, and flour. Beat the eggs, then add the buttermilk and bacon drippings and combine with the dry ingredients. Bake in a 425° oven for 15 to 25 minutes (depends on whether you cook them in cornstick molds or muffin tins).

GOOD FLOATING ISLAND

3   cups medium cream
12 egg yolks
¼   tsp. salt, plus a pinch more
2⅙ cups sugar
2   tbsp. vanilla or liqueur
     (Grand Marnier, Tia Maria
     or rum are good)

To make the custard, whisk together the egg yolks, ¼ teaspoon salt and 1 cup of the sugar until they are just combined. Add the cream and mix well trying not to make any foam. Pour into a heavy-bottomed saucepan and heat over a medium flame. Stir constantly as it will get hot slowly and then thicken quite suddenly. Watch carefully, and as soon as it thickens remove from the heat and pour through a strainer. Whisk till cool. Add the vanilla or liqueur and refrigerate at least an hour. (The custard may be made the day before.)

To make the islands beat the egg whites, with the pinch of salt, until soft peaks are formed. Then add ½ cup sugar and beat until the whites are smooth and stiff.

Now caramelize the remaining sugar. Put ⅔ cup sugar and ½ cup water into a frying pan and cook over a high heat until it foams and bubbles and becomes a golden caramel. Remove immediately from the heat and use as it will continue to darken and become stiff. If it becomes too hard add a little water and warm over a low heat.

Smooth the custard into a low serving dish and spoon the whites on top in blobs to form the islands. Take a fork and dip it into the caramelized sugar. Criss-cross the islands of whites with the caramelized fork, dipping it every time a criss or cross is made.

This dessert can sit finished for about an hour if the egg whites have been beaten enough.

Mixed Bag

Several years ago, Ed and I went smallmouth bass fishing in Maine. I was a novice fisherman and depending on Ed and this trip to change that status. After several easy days of watching an eaglet and his mother, listening to the loons at night and learning about emersion into wilderness, Ed began the campside sessions on casting. Soon enough we paddled down the lake to test the knowledge. Ed made several casts at his chosen spot, caught a fish, threw him back and then pointed to the spot and suggested I give it a try. I remember being disappointed by this learning procedure.

Surely determining where the fish are and catching them because you have made that discovery is one of the most enjoyable aspects of fishing. Ed knew that and has since written quite eloquently in *Gray's Sporting Journal* about the episode. And he is the best of teachers. But even so, instruction has an element of straightforward indoctrination whether it is in fishing, hunting—or cooking.

We have tried to be instructional but not definitive in this book, believing in the need for experimentation and discovery. Unfortunately an imperious tone is too often found in cookbooks, either because the printed word makes it all seem absolute or because the author writes it to sound so. There are no absolutes in cooking game, that is why it is hard and fun to do.

There are also too few game cookbooks where the author confesses to being ignorant on a specific topic. At one point during the writing of this book, Cintra turned to me and said "Well, I'm not the dessert queen, you know." Good as she is, desserts are not her forte. So better to repeat her good recipes than throw in ones we don't know much about (the readers will catch you every time anyway).

I do not know how to cook every type of game. That is why this chapter is thin by comparison to the "Upland Birds," "Water Fowl" and "Venison" chapters. I have tried to write about what I know. And tried to say so when I don't have first-hand knowledge. And tried to leave what I don't know entirely out of the book.

Tempting as it is to try and sound smart about all game cooking, it would be a lie. And I definitely need to reserve my lying for the catching and shooting tales rather than the cooking and eating dissertations.

Roast Leg of Mountain Goat
Blue Cheese Polenta
Mixed Green Salad
Olive Oil and Sauternes Cake

Serves four

ROAST LEG OF MOUNTAIN GOAT

1   leg of goat
2   garlic cloves
½ cup (1 stick) unsalted butter
2   tbsp. rosemary
¼ cup oil

Clean off all fat from the leg with a little knife. Peel and sliver one of the cloves of garlic. Insert, at a slight angle, the slivers of garlic and ¼ teaspoon of the rosemary. Then rub it all with the oil and the rest of the rosemary and let stand in the refrigerator overnight wrapped in foil. Bring to room temperature before roasting. Preheat the oven to 400° and roast for 30 minutes (or about 10 minutes per pound). Then let sit for 15 minutes or so before carving. An hour or even a day before cooking the goat, make a compound butter by whipping together the butter, the last garlic clove chopped fine, and the rosemary, also chopped fine. Salt and pepper to taste. Wrap in plastic wrap and shape into a log, place in the refrigerator. When the leg is ready sprinkle with salt and pepper and serve with the compound butter.

BLUE CHEESE POLENTA

¾   cup cornmeal
1   small onion chopped very fine
    (optional)
2   cups milk
6   tbsp. butter
½   cup heavy cream
5   oz. blue cheese, diced
½   tsp. nutmeg
2–3 tsp. kosher salt
    Pepper

If you are using the onion sauté it in the butter until translucent. Then, in a small saucepan bring the onion, butter and milk to a boil. Add the cornmeal slowly, stirring constantly till thick and the spoon can stand up in it. Be careful as the polenta will spit at you. Remove from the heat. Add the cheese, nutmeg and salt. Beat in the cream and pepper and mix well. Turn immediately into buttered muffin tins and let rest till set. Remove from the tin and put in a heavy oven-proof pan and cook at 400° for 15 minutes (if you like, you can add a little more cheese to the tops of the polenta muffins before putting them in the oven.)

OLIVE OIL AND SAUTERNES CAKE

5 eggs plus 2 egg whites
¾ cup sugar
1 tbsp. mixed grated orange
  and lemon peel
1 cup sifted flour
½ teaspoon salt
½ cup good quality Sauternes
½ cup plus 2 tbsp. extra virgin
  olive oil

Preheat the oven to 375°. Separate the 5 eggs and beat the egg yolks with ¾ cup sugar in a bowl with a whisk for 3 to 5 minutes until light colored and well-beaten. Add the orange and lemon peel and set aside.

Combine 1 cup sifted flour and ½ teaspoon salt, then add bit by bit to the sugar-egg mixture, beating continually until it is all incorporated. Add the Sauternes and olive oil in the same fashion.

Beat the 5 egg whites and 2 additional egg whites until they stand in stiff peaks, then fold them into the mixture thoroughly.

Pour this batter into an 8-inch spring-form pan whose bottom has been lined with parchment and whose entire interior has been well buttered. Bake for 20 minutes, rotating the cake if necessary to insure even cooking. After 20 minutes lower the temperature to 325° and bake for another 20 minutes. Then turn off the oven, cover the cake with a round of parchment, and leave the cake in the closed oven for 10 minutes more while the cake deflates like a fallen soufflé.

Remove the cake from the oven, invert it onto a flat surface, remove from the spring-form pan, allow it to cool completely.

This cake can be stored, well sealed, in the refrigerator. Serve with fresh peaches and a glass of Sauternes.

Braised Bear
Baby Artichokes
Fava Beans, Peas, and Pancetta
Fresh Fruit

Serves four

I have never actually hunted bear although I have cooked it several times and been in camp with bear hunters (we were fishing). We had a bear carcass near our duck camp in Alaska (the local Indians had taken the edible meat and left the rest). And we once came upon some bear hunters while we were hunting partridge.

The bear hunters were tracking with dogs and had an eery resemblance to the folks they hired to do the movie "Deliverance." The dead carcass near our duck camp proved an inconvenience. The two retrievers with us loved to roll in it and then cuddled up at night near us for warmth from the Alaskan fall air. Our bear hunting friends, camping near us while we were landlocked salmon fishing, caused only the greatest of amusement. Left early one morning to huddle over bait (garbage) in hopes of attracting a bear, their guide and only means of getting out of the woods went off...to get drunk. As darkness fell, the hung-over guide tried desperately to remember where he had parked his "sports." The night passed and so did many hours of aimless 4-wheel driving through a lot of the Maine backwoods. The bear hunters were eventually found with black fly bites as big as baseballs and stories of the thrill of sitting over garbage while the springtime sun heated up—and then went ominously down. A little bleary-eyed, but amazingly cheerful. I remember wondering what the appeal was for those bear hunters. Certainly my brief encounters with bear hunting have left me with no great desire to do it.

My bear-*cooking* experiences have, however, been slightly more persuasive—conjuring great images of the lumbering creatures lurking through the wonderful woods of Maine or Michigan or Alaska. The meat must be cooked long (for fear of any possible trichinosis) and therefore is cooked with many herbs, spices and, in this case, much garlic. It is very aromatic—wonderful for the pre-meal anticipation.

This menu is designed for spring bear as it is the only time fava beans or the baby artichokes are available. Also, don't let the amount of garlic scare you. After it cooks for so long it takes on a very mild and sweet flavor.

172

BRAISED BEAR

8   lbs. bear meat cut into 2-inch cubes
40   garlic cloves, peeled
3   carrots
1   large stalk of celery
1   bay leaf
  A few parsley stems
2   tsp. thyme
1   bottle of good red Rhone wine
2   cups veal or chicken stock
1½   sticks of unsalted butter
½   cup corn oil
  Salt and pepper

Brown the meat in the corn oil and set aside. Discard the oil. Chop the onion, carrot and celery and sauté in the same pan as the bear with 2 table-spoons of butter. Add the browned bear meat to the vegetables and pour in the wine and stock. Bring it to a boil and then reduce to a simmer. Add the garlic cloves, thyme and bay leaf to the meat mixture. Cover the pan with foil, pressing down so there is no space between the liquid and the foil and the foil is tight over the sides of the pan. Now cover with the lid and continue simmering until done, about 2–3 hours or when a skewer comes out of a piece of meat easily. Skim off any fat. Remove the meat and discard the bay leaf. Strain the liquid and purée both the liquid and the vegetables in a blender in batches if necessary. Return the mixture to the stove and reduce over a medium heat by ⅓ the quantity. Whisk in the butter and check for salt and pepper. Return the meat to the sauce and reheat for a few minutes. Serve.

BABY ARTICHOKES

8–10 baby artichokes (the very
      small artichokes that are
      about 2 inches long and
      which will have no choke)
      Juice from 1 lemon (3 tbsp.)
3   tbsp. olive oil
1   garlic clove
1   bay leaf
2   tbsp. parsley
½   tsp. thyme
3–4   cups chicken stock
      Salt and pepper

Remove the outer leaves of the artichoke. Trim the top and bottoms and cut each artichoke lengthwise into slices about ¼-inch thick. Keep them in a lemon and water bath while preparing. Chop the parsley and garlic very fine and sauté in olive oil. Add the artichokes, bay leaf, and thyme. Salt and pepper to taste and toss. Pour in the chicken broth so that the chokes are half covered. Simmer with the lid on for 20 minutes turning the artichokes every now and then. Remove the lid and turn up the heat. Stir until the liquid has almost evaporated. Test for seasoning. Place the artichokes on a serving platter and dot with butter. Serve.

FAVA BEANS, PEAS, AND PANCETTA

4 oz. pancetta
2 lbs. fresh peas *or* 1 box frozen
    peas, defrosted (Birdseye's
    Tender Tiny Peas are best)
1 lb. fava beans (these can be
    frozen for 6 weeks or so)

Remove the fava beans from their pods. Peel the outer skin from each bean. This is very tedious and boring but important and worth doing. Steam the beans till barely done, about 5–10 minutes and cool in ice water, then drain. Dice the pancetta into ⅛-inch pieces and sauté over a low heat until it is not quite crispy. Remove it from the pan. Blanch the fresh peas. Put the peas and the fava beans into the pan where the pancetta was and, over a medium flame, heat through. Put into a serving dish, add salt, pepper and pancetta and a little butter and toss.

Boar Chops with Pernod and Mustard Butter
Gaufrette Potatoes
Fiddleheads
Raspberry Tart

Serves four

This menu suggests gaufrette potatoes which requires the use of a man-doline. Another piece of equipment which has an outragious price tag but is very chic. Since what we are really suggesting for this menu are homemade French fries or "chips," you can save the mandoline for when the Queen comes to lunch.

To make the fries you simply slice the potatoes and deep-fat fry them. I make a couple of suggestions: Leave the skin on for a stronger potato flavor, use fresh peanut oil each time (re-use the oil only in desperation) and keep the done fries in the oven while the remainder cook.

BOAR CHOPS WITH PERNOD AND MUSTARD BUTTER

4   boar chops
1½ sticks unsalted butter,
      slightly softened
3   tbsp. Pernod
1   tbsp. good prepared mustard
2   tbsp. oil
      Salt and pepper

Whip the butter until soft, add the mustard, Pernod and salt and pepper to taste. Put into plastic wrap and mold into the shape of a cylinder. Place in the freezer for one hour or overnight. Cook the chops quickly in the oil and season each side with salt and pepper after they have browned. Slice the Pernod butter and serve several pats on top of each chop.

FIDDLEHEADS

1 lb. fiddleheads
3 tbsp. butter
salt and pepper

Cut the stems off the fiddleheads leaving ¾ of the stems. In a large soup pot full of cold water soak the fiddleheads for 5 minutes or so. Then, by the handful, rinse the fiddleheads under the faucet. Pour out the potful of water and repeat the process two or three more times or until the brown chaff has been completely removed. It is very important to remove as much of the chaff as possible because it causes the fiddleheads to be bitter. Bring a quart of salted water to boil and drop in a handful of the fiddleheads. Cook for 3–4 minutes or until they're just tender. Scoop them out and plunge them into ice water to stop the cooking. Drain the fiddleheads in a colander and wrap them in an old towel. Repeat this until you have cooked all the fiddleheads changing the boiling water with each handful of fiddleheads as more chaff will come off in the boiling water. Finally sauté the fiddleheads quickly in the unsalted butter and serve.

RASPBERRY TART

1 sheet Pepperidge Farm Puff Pastry or your own
1 tbsp. butter
2 tbsp. sugar
2 pints raspberries
½ pint heavy cream
2 tbsp. currant jam
½ tbsp. Framboise
3 tbsp. sour cream

Preheat the oven at 425° for at least 20 minutes.

Roll out the pastry and fit into a heavily buttered porcelain tart or quiche dish. Roll the rolling pin over the top to cut the extra pastry off the edges. Let rest in the refrigerator for 1 hour. Prick the pastry with a fork and then flatten a piece of foil tightly over it. Put beans, peas, or pastry weights on top of the foil. Cook in the lower part of the hot oven for 7 minutes then carefully open the oven and remove the foil and weights. Sprinkle with sugar and continue cooking for at least 5 minutes until the crust is a light brown with a shiny, caramelized surface. Then remove from the oven and let cool 1 minute. Slide the pastry out of the dish onto a cake rack to cool completely. Whip the cream. About half way through whipping add the Framboise and the sour cream. Spread over the bottom of the pastry shell. Arrange the raspberries on top of the cream attractively (peaches, blueberries or any fruit are good also). Melt the currant jam over a low flame. Remove and let cool slightly. Add a dash of the liqueur you used in the cream. With a 2-inch pastry brush, paint the raspberries with the jam mixture. Serve immediately as it will become soggy if you try to hold it.

Roast Sheep
Sautéed Watercress
Pasta with Chestnuts and Pignolis
Poached Prunes and Apricots with Cognac and Cream

Serves four

This is one of those menus that whenever I read it I salivate. We had sheep one night on our duck hunting trip in Alaska and the fond memory of it still lingers. Although, in retrospect, I have wondered if this was because we had had Ron Rau's Gizzard Stew and military c-rations (coffee, Type II) the previous evening.

It is all relative, nonetheless. The following is a wonderful meal.

ROAST SHEEP

3–4 lbs. rolled loin roast
2 tbsp. cognac
1½ cups veal stock
1 garlic clove, chopped
Peel from 1 lime, blanched
and julienned
4 tbsp. unsalted butter
2 tbsp. oil

Clean any fat off the roast and brush it with the oil.

Roast the sheep in a hot 450° oven for 1 to 1½ hours according to your taste. Remove the roast from the pan to a warm serving platter. Deglaze the pan with cognac and then add veal stock, chopped garlic and reduce to ½ the amount. Whisk in butter and lime rind. Season with salt and pepper and serve over sliced sheep.

SAUTÉED WATERCRESS

3 bunches of watercress
3–4 tbsp. unsalted butter
Salt and pepper

Take each bunch of watercress and cut into 2-inch lengths (the bunches should be cut approximately into thirds). Sauté the watercress in the hot unsalted butter for a minute or two then add the lid for two minutes. Remove the lid and season with a little more butter and salt and pepper.

PASTA WITH CHESTNUTS AND PIGNOLIS

½ lb. prepared pasta
1 cup heavy cream
¼ cup pignolis
½ lb. chestnuts
2 tbsp. unsalted butter
Salt and pepper
1 tsp. sage

Roast the chestnuts under the broiler till their shells are slightly black and cracked. Let them cool then peel and slice them so you have about ½ cup of chestnuts. Sauté the pignolis in butter till light brown, add the chestnuts and sauté a few minutes more. Reduce the cream by letting it boil slowly in a frying pan till it is halved in quantity then add the sage. Cook the pasta, drain and return it to the cooking pan and toss with the cream. Add the pignolis and chestnuts and check for seasoning.

POACHED PRUNES AND APRICOTS WITH COGNAC AND CREAM

1 bottle of good white wine
12 orange rind slivers
12 lemon rind slivers
½ lb. good quality pitted
and dried prunes
½ lb. dried apricots
1 cup cream
⅛ cup cognac or armangnac
Several cloves

Peel an orange and a lemon with a potato peeler making sure not to get any white pith. Put 12 of the shavings from the orange and 12 from the lemon into a pan with the wine and cloves. Bring the mixture to a boil and let simmer for a few minutes. Add the prunes and apricots, remove from the heat and let sit for 48 hours or more in the refrigerator.

When ready to serve, whip the cream only lightly with the cognac in it and pass with the fruit.

Braised Rabbit
Sautéed Cucumbers
Red Peppers with Basil
Clafoutis

Serves four

Rabbit is shot and eaten more than any other game in this country. I find it quite good, but often very bony. The other problem with rabbit is a disease they carry called tularemia or "rabbit fever." This is transmitted to humans who either eat it or handle an infected rabbit. However, our very knowledgeable friend, Bob Elman, writes in his excellent book, *Hunters Field Guide*, published by Alfred A. Knopf, that the effects of tularemia have been greatly exaggerated. Rarely is the disease fatal (only in about 6% of the cases according to my encyclopedia) and it is easily treated with streptomycin. He does suggest wearing rubber gloves when field dressing a rabbit. And it is advisable to cook the rabbit well. This disease is not reserved for wild rabbits—the friendly butcher shop rabbit can also be infected.

BRAISED RABBIT

1	rabbit	1½	cup wine (about)
4	tbsp. oil	1½	cup stock (about)
1	small onion	1	bay leaf
1	carrot, peeled		Pinch of thyme
½	small celery stick	1	pint heavy cream
6	parsley stems	2	tbsp. dried basil
½	piece bacon or pancetta		Salt and pepper
2	tbsp. unsalted butter		

Cut up the rabbit into pieces and brown quickly in the oil. Remove the oil. Chop the carrot, onion, celery, parsley stems and bacon and sauté in the butter. Add the rabbit pieces, except for the breast, and pour enough wine and stock in equal parts to cover ⅔ of the rabbit. Bring this to a boil, turn down to a simmer, add the thyme and bay leaf and cover with aluminum foil, pressing down and fitting it closely to the rabbit and liquid and bringing it over the sides of the pot for a good seal. Continue cooking on simmer until done (about an hour) or when a skewer inserted into the meat comes out clean. The breast meat should be added to the pot about 10–15 minutes before all is done. Meanwhile, in another pan, reduce the pint of cream to 1 cup and add the basil. Season the cream mixture with salt and pepper and set aside. Remove the rabbit pieces to a warmed serving platter and discard the bay leaf. Strain the liquid and return it to the pan to reduce to half its quantity. Add the reduced basil cream and check for seasoning. Season with salt and pepper and pour over the rabbit.

SAUTÉED CUCUMBERS

8 cucumbers
2 tbsp. unsalted butter
1 tsp. oil
  Sprinkle of dill
  Salt and pepper

Cut and peel the cucumbers in half lengthwise and scoop out the seeds with a teaspoon. Then cut into ¼-inch slices and place in a colander. Sprinkle with salt and let drain for 40 minutes. Rinse the cucumber in cold water. Meanwhile melt the butter in a frying pan and add the oil. When it is hot, add the cucumber and sauté till just tender. Season with salt, pepper and the dill.

RED PEPPER WITH BASIL

2 red peppers, seeded and
  julienned
1 tsp. basil
½ tsp lemon juice
3 tbsp. unsalted butter
  Salt and pepper

Sauté the red pepper in hot butter for just a minute. Add the basil and lemon juice and toss. Season with salt and pepper.

CLAFOUTIS

2 eggs
¾ cup milk
½ cup flour
  Pinch of salt
1 lb. cherries, pitted (any
  fruit is good)
1 tsp. vanilla (or grated lemon
  or orange rind)
¼ cup sugar
  Confectioners' sugar

Mix the flour, milk, vanilla or rind, salt, eggs and 2 tablespoons of the granulated sugar together. Butter an oven-proof serving dish and pour a third of the batter in it. Bake that for 10 minutes at 375°. Remove from the oven and add the fruit and sprinkle with the remaining sugar. Pour in the rest of the batter and continue cooking in the oven for 30 minutes. Sprinkle with confectioners' sugar and cut into pie shape wedges.

Rabbit Salad
Black Olive Bread
Baked Apples with Crème Anglaise

Serves four

RABBIT SALAD

1   rabbit
¼ cup stock
¼ cup walnut oil
2   tbsp. red wine vinegar
1   shallot, chopped fine
2   tbsp. hazelnuts, chopped
2   tbsp. oil
     Salt and pepper
     Bittergreen (chicory, escarole,
     radicchio)

Brush the rabbit with oil and cook in a preheated oven at 350° for about an hour. Remove the rabbit and cut all the meat from the bones and then into bite-size pieces. Now deglaze the pan that the rabbit cooked in with the stock. Turn the heat to low. In a blender, whiz together the vinegar, oil and shallot, taste for salt and pepper, and then add it to the stock in the pan. Toast hazelnuts a few minutes in the oven then wrap in a towel to steam and rub off the skins. Chop coarsely and reserve. Toss the rabbit meat and bittergreens together with the walnut oil and stock mixture. Sprinkle the hazelnuts in and check for salt and pepper. Serve immediately.

BLACK OLIVE BREAD

3   cups all-purpose flour
1   pkg. dry yeast
½   cup pitted black olives
1   tsp. salt
1   tsp. thyme

In a medium-sized bowl mix 1 cup of the flour with the yeast and add enough warm water (not hot water) to make a moist and cohesive ball. Fill the bowl with warm water so the ball is covered. Let sit 5 to 15 minutes until the ball pops to the surface. Meanwhile take the remaining amount of flour (this can be all white flour or a mixture such as ⅔ white and ⅓ whole wheat) and put it on top of the counter. Make a trench in the middle of the pile and add the salt. Chop the olives coarsely and add to the flour trench. Add the thyme. You will also need to add a couple tablespoons of water fluffing it into the flour with your fingers. The mixture should be slightly cohesive but not wet as the yeast/flour ball will be quite wet. When the ball has risen to the surface of the water, scoop it out and set in the middle of your pile of flour. Knead the ball and the flour together and continue to knead for 8 minutes or so. Put the dough in an oiled or floured bowl with a towel over it and place in a warm spot to rise 2 hours or until doubled in bulk. Punch down and let rise again or shape and bake in a preheated oven at 425° till done (about 35–40 minutes). Remember it can rise and be punched down four times, after that the yeast dies. Also, after the first rising it can be punched down and left to rise slowly overnight in the refrigerator.

BAKED APPLES WITH CRÈME ANGLAISE

4   apples
3   tbsp. sugar
     Rind from one orange, blanched
     and julienned
¼   cup raisins
     Pats of butter

For the Crème Anglaise:
½   cup milk
½   cup cream
4 ` yolks
¼   cup sugar
⅛   tsp. salt
1   tbsp. liqueur or vanilla (Grand
     Marnier is good)

Bake the apples first. Combine the sugar, orange peel, and raisins together. Core the apples and cut the peel from the top and bottom. Fill each apple with the raisin mixture and dot the top with butter pats. Bake in a preheated oven at 375° for 40 minutes. While the apples cook, make the crème anglaise. Whisk together the yolks, salt and sugar. Combine the milk and cream and whisk that into the yolks. Cook over a medium-high heat stirring constantly until it thickens quite suddenly. Remove from the heat, strain and then whisk till cool. Add the liqueur or vanilla and spoon the crème anglaise over the cooked apples. Can be served hot or cold.

Boar with Ginger and Orange Sauce
Fried Bread
Fried Sage Leaves
Good Floating Island

Serves four

Fried sage leaves sounds perhaps peculiar but are a delightful taste sensation. The quantitiy suggested here is really only a minimum requirement. If you have more large leaves, use them.

BOAR WITH GINGER AND ORANGE SAUCE

4–5	lbs. roast of boar, cleaned of any fat
	A large sprig of rosemary
¼	cup cognac
2	cups stock (preferably veal)
1	orange, juice and rind peeled with a potato peeler (no white pith)
5	tbsp. unsalted butter
2	tsp. fresh ginger, peeled and julienned.
	Salt and pepper
	Sprigs of watercress

Put the sprig of rosemary in the bottom of the roasting pan and put the boar on top. Roast the boar for 1½ to 2 hours at 325°. Remove the roast to a warm platter. Remove the rosemary.

Deglaze the pan with cognac, add the veal stock and ½ cup of orange juice (be sure to save the rind from the orange). Reduce the liquid by half all the time whisking it. Add the butter and continue whisking. Blanch and julienne the orange rind. Add ginger, orange rind to the veal stock mixture and remove from the heat. Then add any of the juices from the sliced meat and season with salt and pepper. Serve the boar with the sauce and garnish with watercress.

FRIED BREAD

1	loaf French bread
½	cup (1 stick) unsalted butter
	Garlic (optional)

Slice the French bread into 12 ½-inch pieces and dry till stiff in a 300° oven. Rub with garlic if you wish. Do not let them brown. In a heavy-bottomed saucepan, melt the stick of butter heating it till it sizzles. Put in the bread and brown both sides. Sprinkle with salt if you like.

FRIED SAGE LEAVES

½ cup large sage leaves
2 tbsp. unsalted butter

Fry the sage leaves in butter until they're stiff. Remove with wooden tongs and season with salt. Use as a garnish on or around meat, or as an *hors d'oeuvre*.

GOOD FLOATING ISLAND

3 cups medium cream
2⅙ egg yolks
¼ tsp. salt, plus a pinch more
2⅙ cups sugar
2 tbsp. vanilla or liqueur
(Grand Marnier, Tia Maria
or rum are good)

To make the custard whisk together the egg yolks, ¼ teaspoon salt and 1 cup of the sugar until they are just combined. Add the cream and mix well trying not to make any foam. Pour into a heavy-bottomed saucepan and heat over a medium flame. Stir constantly as it will get hot slowly and then thicken quite suddenly. Watch carefully, and as soon as it thickens remove from the heat. Pour through a strainer and whisk till cool. Add the vanilla or liqueur and refrigerate at least an hour. (The custard may be made the day before.)

To make the islands beat the egg whites with the pinch of salt until soft peaks are formed. Then add ½ cup sugar and beat until the whites are smooth and stiff.

Now caramelize the remaining sugar. Put ⅔ cup sugar and ½ cup water into a frying pan and cook over a high heat until it bubbles and turns a pale brown. Remove immediately from the heat and use as it will continue to darken and become stiff. If it becomes too hard add a little water and warm over a low heat.

Smooth the custard into a low serving dish and spoon the whites on top in blobs to form the islands. Take a fork and dip it into the caramelized sugar. Criss-cross the islands of whites with the caramelized fork, dipping it every time a criss or cross is made.

This dessert can sit finished for about an hour if the egg whites have been beaten enough.

Game Care

E d brought home the first deer of our life together—to a Boston apartment. Our small daughter in my arms, we stood on the curb of the city street marveling over the beautiful animal lying across the top of the station wagon. Musing slightly over the incongruity of the situation, I watched as the car disappeared down the dark street bound for the suburban home where it was to be "hung." And the slow realization came over me: "What now?"

At that point I knew only to worry about the obvious mechanics of how to get a whole carcass into the form of cut-up pieces of meat. What I was to learn subsequently was that what had come before the car-top journey and butchering was actually of equal significance and consequence. And worry is what I would have done had I any game care experience. That deer had been through a lot by the time he got to Boston.

He was a particularly large whitetail, about 210 pounds field-dressed, and Ed had shot him in a very remote area. Ed and Larry had worked the better part of a day just to drag the deer back to camp. And then, of course, there was getting it across the stream and onto the roof of the car. The frail, rope footbridge which dangled above the stream did not seem the way to go. On the other hand forging the waist-deep stream with the 210 pounds seemed, at best, un-fun. Weighing the options carefully, the men struck on a somewhat modified rope and pulley system, or the old wrap around the tree trick for accomplishing their task.

With Larry on one side of the stream fixing a rope to the deer's antlers, Ed walked the footbridge with the other end of the rope to wrap around a big tree on the opposite side of the stream. The rope could have been fastened securely there, Larry gone to Ed's side of the river, and the two men could have hauled the beast together or even enlisted the muscle of the car. That could have been the way it worked. It was not. In eager anticipation of Ed's end of the rope being fastened, Larry had dragged the deer close to the stream's edge. And the current's force caused the premature launching of the deer. Gone! Save for those antlers gone forever downstream. The antlers getting hung up on a semi-submerged log proved one more good reason for saving your shots for the trophy rack. A mid-stream wrestling match between Ed, the antlers and the submerged log followed next. Then there was trying to get the deer on top of the car, and driving it eight hours to Boston. A lot had happened to this deer. Fortunately, I didn't know enough to care while standing curb-side in that city street so long ago.

Today I would question every detail of that carcass' history.

What would the day of being pulled through the woods have done to the meat? Did the stream-side bath help or hinder? How did the cold, cold of the water then the warmer air affect the deer? These questions would be coupled with the usual—was it a lung shot, what had the terrain been like, what was his probable diet and age? And every bite of that deer's meat would have been scrutinized and some conclusion drawn about the taste and tenderness attributable to the deer's history. What a general pain in the neck I would have made of myself. But all those elements can in fact, or according to folk lore anyway, affect the meat.

What is fact and what is myth? Much has been written in game cookbooks and in the outdoor literature about how different elements and field and kitchen affect the taste of what you are eating. It always has been very hard for me to discern what is simply the opinion of the writer (or is included more for the sake of tradition) and what is reason. I wanted scientific reasons for why venison must be hung and for how long, head up or down, etc. Fortunately, coming from a family of meat-packers and food technologists, I have had some sources to question.

My father is a chemical engineer who has spent 35 years in the food industry specializing in food processing and meat packing in scores of countries around the world. Here is restated some of the information he has provided me about the care and treatment of meat.

About freezing: Of course, the first consequence of freezing is that it cuts down on bacteria growth and allows us to keep the meat for a long time. At the same time it has several other consequences. Meat has a very high water content—over 65%. Freezing causes the globules of water cells to crystallize. The size of the crystals is in inverse proportion to the speed of freezing. If the freezing occurs quickly the crystals will be quite small. If the freezing happens slowly the crystals will be quite large and cause any yet-unfrozen water to exude out of the meat. In addition, as the temperature is lowered expansion of the water cells occurrs and may cause a bursting of the cells if done slowly. Consequently, slow freezing can cause the meat to lose moisture and also become mushy. Slow thawing, as in a refrigerator, may have a similar effect. As the temperature of the refrigerator goes up and down the cells may crystallize and then liquify causing the same bursting and exuding of moisture. The blowers inside frost-free freezers, or any air movement, can cause freezer burn—a desiccation of the meat.

All that this suggests is that if meat is going to be frozen it should be done as quickly as possible, well wrapped and then thawed quickly (or at least at a consistently warm temperature). The suggested wrap for frozen meat is a first layer of aluminum foil to obtain rapid heat transfer and protection from air and then 12 hours later a second wrap of a plastic bag to protect further against air movement. Added tips are to press the foil tightly around the meat. Remember to label, date, and grade the piece and when the baggie goes over it to suck the air out before the twist-tie goes on. The labeling, of course, helps you know what you're cooking before you've thawed it. Nothing worse than to plan an *ooh la la* dinner and then discover you've thawed that shot-up shoveler that's been in the freezer a year (almost all meat has significantly deteriorated after a year of the freezer).

About smoking meat: A hot smoking of meat, like freezing, has the effect of cutting down on the bacteria growth, allowing the meat to be kept longer. Smoking does three things to meat: it heats it, dries it and adds flavor to it. The long, slow heating process of smoking brings the temperature of the meat to above 127 degrees or the "denaturing point." This changes the color of the meat from blood red and kills some, but not all, of the bacteria. The meat also becomes firmer. The drying cuts the moisture content and makes the meat less hospitable to bacteria, while the addition of the smoked flavor adds some acidity, making it even more difficult for certain bacteria to grow. The amount of time a piece of smoked meat can be kept depends largely on the effectiveness of the heating, drying and flavoring process. This may be difficult to determine. Often we don't know much about how well a piece of meat has been smoked or how long it's been hanging around since the smoking. The guidelines are perhaps to be found in the two extremes. A Smithfield ham can be kept for months, even years, unrefrigerated; something you smoke yourself in the backyard can probably go as long as a month in the refrigerator and probably six months to a year in the freezer. Fortunately, meat is quite forgiving. And, as my father would say, and it will let you know when it's had it.

About hanging meat: Hanging meat, or aging it, tenderizes it. The aging process begins after rigor mortis has peaked. Rigor mortis begins a few hours after the animal has been shot and increases very rapidly, peaking at about 10 to 24 hours. It then will decline with the curve flattening at about 48 hours and will continue to decline for two weeks. The meat will be at its toughest stage during rigor mortis and then it will become increasingly more tender. The amount of time for aging to occur is significantly affected by temperature. This is why the location of your hunt has a great deal to do with how long the meat should be hung and how it should be handled right after shooting it. In general, the higher the temperature the faster the aging process and the softer the meat. Of course, if the temperature is too high growth of bacteria is promoted, too. Consequently how long an animal should be hung has to do with your own taste buds and the temperature control over the period of aging (a good regulated temperature of 45–50 degrees is optimum).

Taste being the key, it is difficult to advise in such matters. But since much of what is found acceptable is based on what Americans are used to, the guideline might start at what is desirable for beef, and in this country all beef is aged about two weeks.

We age our venison anywhere from a week to two, depending on the weather and how long the temperatures have held steady. This, of course, is the bottom line for us. If not rigged with a cooler, the length of time for aging becomes somewhat a function of what the weatherman dictates and has not much to do with what has been advised or found to be most desirable.

About cleaning the meat: In our culture the taste of blood is generally not well received and some lengths should be gone to to clean the animal properly if you wish to comply with cultural norms. Of course, the hunter can always help by trying for a lung shot on the bigger animals such as a deer. The lung shot will guarantee the least amount of damage, blood or otherwise, to the meat, and also kill the animal quickly. Hanging the animal for aging or butchering with the head to the ground is suggested for cleanliness sake. A spraying with hot water before freezing or refrigeration is also advisable for meat in order to keep down the bacteria count. Use paper towel to pat the meat dry rather than the kitchen dish towel (no need to add the bacteria from the towel back into the meat).

Other things which can affect the flavor of the meat: Age, size and even sex of the animal can affect the taste of the glandular meat (neck and shoulder meat). An old, big female is likely to have tougher, stronger flavored neck meat than the saddle from a young, small buck.

Fat contains the flavor of what the animal has been eating and will flavor the meat if left on while cooking.

To soak meat in water, salted water or milk causes some exuding of flavor from the meat. Then, after the exuding, the flavor of the salt and milk will mask what the animal has been feeding on.

The effect of cooking: The purpose of cooking a piece of meat is to render it more digestible and to eliminate any diseases. The specifics of how something is cooked get into a matter of taste, of course, but certain generalizations can be made. The longer and slower meat is cooked the more tender and easily digestible it becomes (it also loses more of the vitamins). The higher and shorter the heat the juicier the meat and the crisper the skin. Finally, to cook a bird "in the round" probably does nothing to the taste of the meat. It probably does make the innards more convenient to eat if you like them. One word of caution, however, on this. Innards, particularly the liver, are the body's depository for several types of chemicals that animals feed on. In this insecticide-laden society that is worth remembering.

So how to know the taste. You can't. You can know that a neck roast from a big, old, bark-eating female deer with blood and fat all over it and cooked ten hours after it was shot or a year after being in the freezer, unwrapped, then cooked on a high heat for a long time won't taste very good. But hopefully you knew that before you read this. Every time an element is altered, the taste is altered. And what must be kept in perspective are those elements which you have some control over. Hopefully the generalized facts listed above which determine flavor and texture will help you determine what things you are going to strive to control. It is possible to control the temperature for hanging by purchasing your very own $10,000 meat locker. It is possible to break the law and shoot a springtime buck. It is possible to eat only the saddle roast from a deer dead one hour. All these things are possible, but often impractical or illegal or unfun. Focus on what suits you to control and beware of the risks when you do cut corners. Certainly the height of control is to make the meat into what we eat every day: created, maintained, slaughtered and packaged meat with a predictable flavor. Hopefully the adventurous spirit in you is willing to try to eat and cook what the hunter presents. Be smart and energetic when preserving and cooking game, but also willing to improvise when a lack of ideal circumstances or utensils dictates it.

Lastly, remember that in the final analysis what often constitutes proper game care is usually linked to what makes the meat taste "good." And what constitutes "good" in taste is not always agreed upon.

There's More to a Menu Than the Game

Many times the design of my menus has more to do with the chaos that is occurring in my life that day than the ingredients I have on hand or what my mood might dictate. If I have been hunting all day and want a fast, easy game meal I might choose one set of recipes over the ones that I save for the Annual Event or for the intimate candle-lit dinner for two. This is true, I believe, of all of us. So we have re-shuffled all the menus in the preceding chapters and list them here in accordance with the occasion.

Menus for After a Day of Hunting

Or whatever it is that is filling your day. These are, for the most part, quick and easy menus. Planned for immediate assembly, or for making ahead. But take care because several of the ingredients may not be something that you casually stock.

· **Grilled Venison Chops with Blue Cheese and Caraway Seeds**
Sweet Potato Gratin
Braised Fennel
Fresh Figs

Venison Scallops
Persillade Potatoes
Green Beans
Tarte Tatin

Duck Roasted with Red Pepper Butter
Persillade Potatoes
Sautéed Green Beans and Cherry Tomatoes
Almond Cake

Stuffed Duck Breasts
Green Beans and Wild Mushrooms
Bibb and Radish Salad
Grapefruit Sabayon

Woodcock Armagnac
Fennel and Peas
Roast Potatoes
Garlic Toasts
Tarte Tatin

Duck with Ginger and Scallions
Sautéed Watercress
Cheese, Thyme Toasts
Chocolate Cake

Venison Strip Steaks
Fried Potato Skins
Red Pepper Salad
Strawberry Ice Cream

Sea Duck With Pancetta and Prosciutto
Roast Potatoes with Rosemary
Fresh Green Peas
Kiwi Ice

Quail Soup
Pasta with Chestnuts and Pignolis
Olive Oil and Salt Bread

Spitted Woodcock
Green Beans with Wild Mushrooms
Peach and Pear Ice with Crystallized Viol

Grilled Quail
Purée of Peas
Grilled Mushrooms
Pear Cake

Menus For the Great Outdoors

Several of these menus, with some minor adaptation, could be suitable for the first or second night out on a camping trip. They are not the filler-up-fuel type meals but rather the kind which celebrate the beginning of a hunting trip. Consider carefully, as some of the recipes call for a fair amount of refrigerated food and your cooler may not be able to handle it on a particular trip. Or some may simply be more suitable for the evening back at home, standing with cocktail in hand over the barbecue and gazing off, remembering the trip past.

Charcoal Grilled Venison Steaks with Rosemary Butter
Bibb Lettuce and Tomato Salad
White Bean Purée
Coffee Ice Cream and Hazelnut Liqueur

Venison Steaks with Wild Mushrooms
Blue Cheese Polenta
Spinach and Bibb Lettuce Salad
Strawberry Ice

Sea Duck with Anchovy Butter
Olive Oil and Salt Bread
Soup in a Pumpkin
Figs in Rum

Grilled Breast of Mallard
Gorganzola Polenta
Cucumbers and Radishes
Fresh Fruit

Quick Charcoal Quail
Cauliflower and Mayonnaise
Sautéed Watercress
Chocolate Cake

Pheasant and Ruffed Grouse Sandwiches
Cold Wild Rice Salad
Assorted Cheeses
Olives
Fresh Fruit

Grouse Pancetta
Julienned Celery and Zucchini
Fried Polenta
Poached Prunes and Apricots with Cognac and Cream

Quail for the Campfire
Grilled Red Onion
Charcoal Grilled Bread
Almond Cake

Menus That Are *Ooh La La*

No matter how much game you shoot, it is always special. These menus are for the silver, the game plates, the linen, the cognac and, in general, for making life a little bit more elegant.

Boar with Ginger and Orange Sauce
Fried Bread
Fried Sage Leaves
Good Floating Island

Venison with Port
Roast Potatoes
Sautéed Watercress
Peach and Pear Ice with Crystallized Violets

Preserved Woodcock with Olives
Basil Pasta
Sun-dried Tomato Bread
Cantaloupe Ice

Roast Turkey
Fontina Polenta
Fava Beans, Peas, and Pancetta
Green Salad
Rhubarb Tart

Smoked Goose Salad
Butternut Squash Soup
Sun-dried Tomato Bread
Chocolate Cake

Christmas Goose Anytime
Pignolis and Raisin Cognac Stuffing
Cornsticks
Sautéed Bittergreens
Good Floating Island

Saddle of Venison
Potatoes and Porcini
Braised Fennel
Clafoutis

Roast Leg of Goat
Blue Cheese Polenta
Mixed Green Salad
Olive Oil and Sauternes Cake

Boar Chops with Pernod and Mustard Butter
Gaufrette Potatoes
Fiddleheads
Raspberry Tart

Roasted Sheep
Sautéed Watercress
Pasta with Chestnuts and Pignolis
Poached Prunes and Apricots with Cognac and Cream

Menus for People Who Have Never Eaten Game and Don't Eat Things That Walk Sideways or Grow In the Dark

In general, it is probably a bad idea to serve game to the untested palate. Certainly there is nothing so depressing as serving a perfect little grouse just to have it slipped to the dog or shoved under the mashed potatoes. However, there are unavoidable occasions when the unexpected guest arrives after the evening's meal has been pulled from the freezer or when you simply must cater first to your own desires and the guests be hanged. These menus are for those occasions. They will either mask slightly the game taste or utilize the more familiar game that the novice will feel comfortable eating.

Venison Calzone
Sliced Tomatoes with Basil
Fried Sage Leaves
Poached Pears

Venison Steak with Red Wine
Bittergreens and Cheese Salad
Garlic Toasts
Rhubarb Tart

Venison Steaks Marinated
Grilled Red Pepper Salad
Mashed Potatoes with Fresh Basil
Vanilla Ice Cream with Homemade Butterscotch Sauce

Venison Stew with Artichoke Hearts and Sun-dried Tomatoes
Basil Bread
Green Salad
Custard Oranges

Chateaubriand Butter with Venison Burgers
Fried Bread
Vegetable Salad
Fresh Fruit

Marinated Duck Breasts
Plain Roast Potatoes
Julienned Celery and Zucchini
Strawberry Tart

Grilled Marinated Ducks
Grilled Red Onion
Grilled Mushrooms
Basil Bread
Crème Brulée

Pheasant Salad
Soup in a Pumpkin
Basil Bread
Figs in Rum

Roasted Duck
Potatoes Steamed with Sage
Bittergreens and Cheese Salad
Tangerine Sorbet

Minted Dove
Leg of Lamb
White Bean Purée
Green Salad
Stuffed Oranges

Just For the Two Of You

In our hunting careers there have been times when all that the season produced was a meal for two. We plan an evening of candlelight, a late dinner and a very expensive bottle of wine suited to our precious piece of game. Other seasons the meals for two continue, even if we shoot enough for a party.

Venison Chops with Basil Cream
Homemade Pasta with Parsley
Salad with Hazelnut Dressing
Brandied Apricots and Crème Anglaise

Venison Chops with Mustard Butter
Roast Potatoes with Rosemary
Green Beans and Beet Salad
Coffee Granita

Venison Chops with Pignolis and Red Peppers
Pepperoni Bread
Green Salad
Stuffed Oranges

Grilled Lemon Duck
Grated Zucchini
Sautéed Cherry Tomatoes
Charcoal Grilled Bread
Pear Cake

Minted Roast Duck, Carrots and Turnips
Green Salad
Olive Oil and Sauternes Cake

Ducks with Rosemary and Sage
Fontina Polenta
Zucchini Fans with Tomatoes
Coffee Ice Cream and Frangelico

Chukar Stuffed with Hazelnuts
Grated Zucchini
Sautéed Cherry Tomatoes
Cheese Thyme Toasts
Fresh Fruit

Pheasant in Wine
Fiddleheads
Baked Grits
Strawberry Tart

Green Grape Quail
Wild Rice with Walnuts
Sliced Tomatoes with Fresh Basil
Crème Brulée

Dove Salad
Cornsticks
Tangerine Sorbet

And to Feed an Army or Hunting Party...

These menus suggest what types of game are best suited for feeding a big group. No sense in saving up for six hunting seasons trying to have enough woodcock to feed the skeet club when there's a deer in the freezer.

Braised Bear
Baby Artichokes
Fava Beans, Peas, and Pancetta
Fresh Fruit

Rabbit Salad
Black Olive Bread
Baked Apples with Crème Anglaise

Braised Rabbit
Sautéed Cucumbers
Red Peppers with Basil
Clafoutis

Venison Stew
Homemade Pasta
Crusted Blueberry and Cream Cake

Smoked Goose in Cold Pasta Salad
Pepperoni Bread
Almond Cake

Sea Duck Fricassee
Fennel, Mint, Cucumber, Radish Salad
Fried Polenta
Fresh Fruit

Duck Salad
Basil Pasta
Cantaloupe Ice

Grilled Sea Ducks
Grilled Vegetables
Garlic Cheese Bread
Poached Pears

Pheasant and Cabbage
Cooked Apples
Cheese

Fried Dove
Zucchini with Tomato
Gorganzola Polenta
Toll House Cookies

A Few Suggestions

When I first started to cook game, and to read game cookbooks, I automatically skipped over this type of chapter. After all, I knew how to cook and I could see on their list of necessary utensils such items as "pepper grinder." What an insult! Of course, a few game dinner failures would send me lurking into the bathroom, four game cookbooks at a time, to surreptitiously read every "tips" section I could lay my hands on.

Certainly much of what has been said in this book is not new or edifying. Just as many of the recipes are not "new." Many of the suggestions and non-game recipes are reiterated in some other place in the book. This is not because I think you didn't get it or perhaps that you didn't even know it before, it is because I believe people read cookbooks differently. If you are like me you have used recipes, maybe a whole menu here and there, long before reading any of the long text chapters. So for the reader like myself there are the suggestions woven around the edges of each menu. For the Cintra types (who actually read a cookbook while standing on one leg in the bookstore) or for those insecure moments when you panic and will read anything with the word "game" in it, there is this chapter. We've tried to present the information in such a way as to please and ease your brain and eye, as well as your palate, no matter what kind of cookbook reader you are.

There is another reason for the repetition. What we want to impart to you is not simply a series of recipes but rather a series of techniques, an attitude about cooking game which will spark you and provide a reliable base for you to build your own creations. But of course the techniques must be known by rote for the creations to have a hope of being successful. And repetition is the handmaiden to rote learning.

For more years than I care to admit to I was afraid to go hunting by myself. Without my husband to direct me around the marsh in the dark or handle the dog I was convinced I was incapable of survival afield. But as the impracticality of always hunting together (who can find a babysitter other than a husband at 4:30 in the morning) became more apparent, I knew I must learn to venture out alone. My hunting attire laid out the night before to prevent darkroom fumble, I was releasing the dog from his pen not more than ten minutes after the alarm had gone off. With six checks to my breast pocket for my license, another reexamination of the shells in each side pocket (duck loads in the right side, goose loads in the left), I was happy I had not spent the time to stop for coffee—I certainly didn't need the extra buzz. There was a half-hour's drive to the marsh and then a ten minute marsh walk for this morning pass shoot at black ducks. There sure seemed to be more ditches in the marsh to cross than I remembered and it did seem unusually dark. I realized that I had forgotten to borrow Ed's watch with the little light in it so I would know when the legal shooting time had arrived. I'd have to estimate the length of time which had transpired from my last glance at the car clock. I could do that, couldn't I? (What a Doubting Dolly I was becoming). I waited in my spot and heard the whistle of wings and saw the speeding dots pass before me. It must be time now. The dog was quivering next to me. I saw the perfect shot coming. I fired and the duck tumbled and bounced on the ground—across the big creek. I sent the dog. But the dog was not trained to do his fancy retrieves, like across the big creek, for me, only for Ed. And I had to send him again and again. When the dog finally made it to the other side of the creek he couldn't find the duck. And then I began to doubt where I thought it had fallen, and then to doubt that I had even seen it fall. Maybe I'd shot at an illegal time. It was dark and my eyes played funny, anticipatory tricks in that light and with those high expectations. What made matters worse is that I had spent so much time trying to get the dog to do the retrieving that I had allowed the tide to come up in the creek to the point of being totally uncrossable in my hip-boots. Now I had to go find a boat. I spent the next hour or so borrowing a friend's boat, paddling to the other side of the creek and scouting for my duck. It would have been so nice if my first time out alone I had come back with dinner. But it was not to be. The friend who lent me the boat did tell me sometime later that their dog had found a half disintegrated duck in that part of the marsh several days later. Maybe it was mine.

I had hunted that marsh for three years with Ed before doing it myself. Nothing could have been more mechanical. But of course nothing interesting in life is truly mechanical. The duck will fall in a difficult location to reach, the dog will balk at the directions, the phone will ring in the middle of rolling out the pastry dough, the child will demand attention when the venison is ready to serve. Practice has only made it all as good as it can be. And these menus cannot guarantee that you will reach the total Nirvana of perfectly executed game dinners without still having some moments of doubt. Let this listing of suggestions at least offer you the security that basically you know what you're doing.

Game dinners cannot always be planned well in advance. When the first bird of the season has been shot and it seems sacrilege to freeze him, this is not the time to start ordering walnut oil from a catalog or searching your gourmet shops for porcini mushrooms. And certainly alongside the importance of practicing good techniques should be the stress on using good ingredients. The time and money is worth it to bettering the meal and is the very least a cook can do. Remember the hunter has probably spent three times the money and time to get the critter to the kitchen than you have by stocking good brandy.

For me the fall season becomes a time for "laying in" supplies and "putting up" homemade items to assist when preparing game. This preparation will also make the cooking of game menus very easy.

Here are some things to buy and keep around:

Fresh herbs–Buy the little plants that come in cheap plastic containers for a few dollars and use the leaves without care or worry to the health of the plant. When the leaves are gone, buy another plant.

Dried wild mushrooms–Most gourmet shops have them and their earthy taste goes much better with the flavor of game than the rubber mushrooms found in grocery stores.

Unsalted butter–Salt was used to mask flavor. We don't want to mask flavor and don't need to add salt to the diet. So better to use unsalted butter.

Birdseye Tender Tiny Peas–They are almost as good as the fresh ones.

Pepperidge Farm Pastry Sheets–This is the best store-bought pastry dough. (But still will not compare to well-made, homemade pastry.)

Good cooking oils–A good, green olive oil, a walnut or a hazelnut oil are good oils and can be purchased through catalogs and in gourmet shops. The walnut oil and hazelnut oils will go rancid if you don't use them up after five months or so. Since it is expensive it might be worth finding a friend to split a bottle with.

Sun-dried tomatoes–Cintra and I have arguments about exactly how difficult to find, and expensive, sun-dried tomatoes are. I think very and she thinks not at all. In either case they are so wonderful and have so many uses, they're worth accumulating no matter what. They can be found in gourmet shops or Italian grocery stores.

Wild rice–Wild rice is a classic with game and always a good idea to have around. I don't care for the mixed brown and wild rice, but this is a matter of taste.

Interesting liqueurs and brandy–They will turn a dull item into something very interesting and are fun to play with.

Juniper berries–These seem to be listed in every game cookbook and are among the items I think worth laying in.

Here are some things to make and keep around:

Veal stock–It is worth it, it is worth it, it is worth it. Veal stock would probably make horse meat taste good. It cannot be bought. It can be frozen.

Chicken stock–Although chicken stock can be bought, it is better home-made; it has less salt for one thing. If you must buy chicken stock and live in an area where College Inn brand is available, we recommend it.

Jellies–Good homemade jellies add not only an oft-needed taste but style to an otherwise flat game dinner. Two of my favorites are beach plum and rose-hip.

Breads–Having homemade herb bread around can do the same as the homemade jellies—really add class to the meal. Squishy white bread does not seem to have the same effect.

Compound butter–Several different compond butters are listed in this book and all can be kept in the freezer for at least a couple weeks. They are good for those last-minute attempts at making a dinner *ooh la la*. Also, provides a good vehicle for freezing some of the hard-to-get fresh herbs.

Homemade mayonnaise–This is good to have on hand to use on leftover game.

MAYONNAISE

3 egg yolks
1 tbsp. vinegar
2 tsp. prepared mustard
½ tsp. salt
¼ tsp. ground pepper
2 cups oil (olive or corn oil)

In a bowl put vinegar, mustard, salt and pepper. Whisk to dissolve the salt. Add the egg yolks and whisk 1 minute till frothy. Add the oil very slowly, in dribbles, whisking all the while. Dribble the oil in for at least the first ½ cup. You may add it faster as the mayonnaise thickens. If the mixture is too thick, add a little hot water to thin. This will also slightly poach the eggs and keep the mayonnaise from separating. When all is combined you have a mayonnaise which now can be seasoned to your own taste. Adjust the salt, pepper and mustard. It is now mayonnaise and you may consider adding lemon juice, herbs, parsley or watercress. Be sure to combine any added herbs in warm water as they will not dissolve in all that oil.

What equipment to obtain is, I believe, truly a personal decision. In general terms I don't believe in purchasing expensive equipment until the level of use warrants the cost. It irritates me when I watch professional cooks on television dictate to me how to poach a salmon when they are casually heaving around their 3 ½-foot long poacher. Very few people have a 3 ½-foot long poacher or the stove to accommodate it, much less the wherewithal to purchase such items. Better the t.v. cook should tell us how to poach in the dishwasher or use the turkey roaster. There are a few items, however, which are important to know about because of their particular usefulness with game. These I list below.

Good poultry shears–These are a handy item not only for cutting up cooked birds but for cleaning a bird (cuts off feet and neck).

Strawberry huller–These are nice little pinchers that are designed to pull the green tops off strawberries, but actually seem better suited to pulling the pinfeathers out of early-season ducks.

Small roasting pans–In general, meat cooks better in a pan which nicely accomodates it, not too big or small. One woodcock in a turkey roaster doesn't work well at all. Since many game birds are smaller than grocery store birds it may be necessary to acquire an especially small roasting pan.

Good sharp knives–A good set of very sharp knives sounds like the pepper grinder suggestion. But I cannot overstress how much more pleasant working on a piece of meat can be if done with a variety of sizes of sharp knives that are well suited to your hand. When John Hewitt comes to visit his house present is to sharpen my knives and no better present could there be.

Meat grinders–Many game cookbooks contain recipes for venison sausage or ground venison burger. Easy for them to talk about. I spent one whole evening till 12:30 at night trying to get venison through my handy-dandy meat grinder. I think I ended up in tears, but I learned several things. I had chosen the mediocre leg and upper neck pieces to grind which contain a great deal of sinew. A logical choice since those cuts are not good for much else. But just as we would have a difficult time chewing that meat so did the grinder. A big meatlocker operation has a machine which actually removes the sinew first. Using a better cut of meat, unaged and never frozen (so it would not be tender or mushy), and fitting the grinder with sharper blades and a tighter fitting plate might have made the procedure possible. But much easier is to hand chop the meat or put it in the foodprocessor. Or better still, con some butcher to do it for you.

Smokers–Now that I have made the statement that I don't appreciate books and professional cooks recommending cooking methods which require expensive equipment, I will make the exception. I think smokers are great fun for cooking game and I suggest buying one even if you can't see using it very much. Yes, yes I say don't buy until you're sure of the amount of usage the equipment will get, and we all do own twice as much stuff as we need. But smokers add an entirely new dimension to the taste of game (unlike such items as an electric plucker), can double as an outdoor grill and be used for other than game meat. I think you'll find it is used more than anticipated.

Two general suggestions to bear in mind about equipment:

Foodprocessors–These handy machines should be used sparingly on starches, only an occasional zip here, zip there. They can break down starches so they are liquified and lose any thickening capability. This is most significant to keep in mind when making a soup when rice or pasta is used specifically to thicken.

Ovens cook very differently–You, undoubtedly, have heard this before, but I have been particularly reminded of it when setting the cooking times for the recipes in this book. Cintra and I almost had a row over the cooking time for crème brulée due (I think) to the differences in our ovens. She kept reiterating that crème brulée is to be just barely firm, not, as some chefs suggest, pudding-like. I knew that, but my cooking time was still 10 minutes longer than she had suggested in the recipe and I found it nearly impossible to caramelize the brown sugar on top. I've cooked in ovens that take a long time to heat up, that don't retain the heat, and never get super hot—all these factors effect the total amount of time something cooks and underlines the necessity of preheating and perhaps even using an auxilary thermometer.

Once the suitable ingredients and equipment are assembled there are those happy moments in the kitchen. There are also those unhappy moments in the kitchen. I always feel particularly bad when a game dinner doesn't come out. It seems such a waste. But everyone, yes everyone, has failures. Cintra taught me early on to pretend that the "failure" was actually something you meant to do and that with a little doctoring it will be as good or better than the original recipe. Very sound advice—but some of my failures have been beyond all repair. To aid in the prevention of failure we make a few suggestions:

Game birds should always be trussed. They just don't have enough fat content to be cooked with an open cavity.

Game continues to cook after it has been removed from the heat. This is, of course, true of all things, but particularly true of the high-in-protein/low-in-fat ratio of game.

A good rule of thumb is the smaller the bird the higher the oven temperature.

Precisely because ovens do vary in their cooking characteristics it is wise to learn to determine the doneness of meat by touch (springiness when pressed or looseness of a leg), smell (you know when its beginning to burn) and sight (coloring and nice oozing juices). To rely on a recipe's stated time for cooking should be for the purposes of determining an approximate length for the cocktail hour and not much more.

Salt and pepper are more effective as flavoring if added after cooking.

Simmering is the waltz, boiling the polka. You should see only an occasional bubble when simmering.

You can always cook something more, but not less.

To "butterfly" a bird is to do this:

What you want to achieve here is a flattened bird with a uniform thickness. First cut out the backbone entirely, then bend the legs and wings as illustrated and insert the leg ends into two slits you have cut just below the breast meat. Press down on the entire bird to flatten. There should be no need to snap the keel bone in a smaller bird.

The purpose of butterflying is to make the cooking more even and speedier.

Stuffing a bird has the effect of putting a sponge in it. If the stuffing is dry, juices will be sucked from the bird. This may be desirable if the bird was poorly cleaned or particularly bloody. If the stuffing is very moist it can add juices. Unless the bird's cavity was immaculately clean, I suggest eating stuffing that has been cooked separately.

Many general cookbooks that contain game recipes are often referring to pen-raised game rather than wild game. The techniques and cooking times are in certain cases quite different from the pen-raised to the wild and this should be accounted for. Ducks and geese most noticeably so; the pen-raised variety are fatty and often very greasy. This is not true of a properly cleaned wild duck or goose.

For some reason game more than other meat seems to cool down very quickly so it is particularly important to serve game on heated plates and platters.

Serving a reasonably sized portion arranged in a careful and pretty fashion on the plate is one of those signs that says you know what you're doing. Just as the color photographs in this book have been added to create a feeling of sensuality and ambiance rather than instruction, this also is the purpose, I think, of a beautifully presented meal.

Many fine and long-time hunters never truly become able to create their own hunting expeditions. They are perfectly capable of hiring guides, and following through the woods and pulling the trigger or simply following in the footsteps of grandfather. It is becoming a rarer commodity to find the hunter who can figure out new territory to hunt and persist in hunting there until the whereabouts of the game is consistently known. This ability takes much time for sure; I have yet to accomplish it. Certainly, too, there are many fine cooks that produce wonderful meals by simply following the recipes. But for me the greatest fun is in the new creation, the improvised and the successful experiment. It is also why the nature of game cooking—unstructured, unpredictable and full of room to create—is so exciting to me. I only hope that my excitement is yours, too.

Index

213

steak with wild mushrooms,
48
stew, 31, 35
strip steaks, 28
with port, 38
Venison Calzone, 62
Venison Chops with Basil
Cream, 64
Venison Chops with Mustard
Butter, 45
Venison Chops with Pignolis and
Red Peppers, 42
Venison Scallops, 40
Venison Steak with Red Wine,
58
Venison Steaks Marinated, 51
Venison Steaks with Wild
Mushrooms, 48
Venison Stew, 31
Venison Stew with Artichoke
Hearts and Sun-dried
Tomatoes, 35
Venison Strip Steaks, 28
Venison with Port, 38

Watercress
sautéed, 38
White Bean Purée, 55

Widgeon (see Water Fowl, 119)
marinated, 133
Wild Rice with Walnuts, 74
Wild rice
salad, 95
with walnuts, 74
Wild mushrooms
about, 207, 78
green beans and, 79
potatoes and porcini, 25
with venison, 48
Wood ducks (see Water Fowl,
119)
grilled with lemon, 153
Woodcock
preserved with olives, 85
spitted, 78
with armagnac, 112
Woodcock Armagnac, 112

Zucchini
grated, 115
with julienned celery, 76
with tomatoes, 84
Zucchini Fans with Tomatoes,
123
Zucchini with Tomato, 84

This book was designed by DeCourcy Taylor Jr.
The type is Caslon 540 and was set by DEKR
    Corporation, Woburn, Massachusetts
The color separations were made by Uni •
    Graphic • Inc., Saugus, Massachusetts
The paper is Moistrite Web
The printing and binding was by The Alpine
    Press, Inc., Stoughton, Massachusetts